EVERYBODY'S MARIONETTE BOOK

EVERYBODY'S MARIONETTE BOOK

WRITTEN AND ILLUSTRATED
BY
H. W. WHANSLAW

AUTHOR OF
"EVERYBODY'S THEATRE,"
"BANKSIDE BOOK OF PUPPETS," ETC.

LONDON:
WELLS GARDNER, DARTON AND CO., LTD.
PATERNOSTER BUILDINGS, E.C. 4.

PRINTED IN GREAT BRITAIN
WELLS GARDNER, DARTON & CO., LTD.

CONTENTS

LIST OF ILLUSTRATIONS

ILLUSTRATIONS—*continued.*

ILLUSTRATIONS—*continued.*

Everybody's Marionette Book

CHAPTER I

BY WAY OF INTRODUCTION

AT the outset let it be clearly understood that any reference to "professionals" in this book, means, not only that class of operators who are called by the name of "showmen," who produce and manage their marionette theatres as a definitely business proposition, but *anybody* and *everybody* who might wish to make use of marionettes for any special purpose in the course of their employment or business career:—school teachers, educational lecturers, advertising experts, film producers, as well as the ordinary individual who turns to puppetry for his own personal pleasure and amusement.

The aim of the author is to set out in this book the ways and means of making and producing a puppet theatre on modern lines, and of a practical type, fit for professional use in which all the "tricks of the trade," so to speak, are embodied. Where the dolls *will do* what the operator hopes of them, and the producer may feel confident that his scenery and lighting will not fail him and his stage in particular will never *let him down*.

The business of puppetry is a vastly different affair to-day to what it was when the old-time showmen erected their rickety "fit-ups" at fairs and other jubilations, when rough-and-tumble dolls, chopped out in the crudest of manners from any old bit of wood that came to hand, with flimsy joints and hideous make-up, jigged and "floated" about, more often in the air than on the stage, when rushlight, penny "dip," and kerosene lamps were the only means of illumination.

In the earlier days, when Flocton and Powell and Pinkethman drew their crowds, artists gave their time and talents to the task of producing dolls that were wonderful works of art like those of the Venetian Court Theatre now in the Victoria and Albert Museum. When the popularity of the marionette began to wane, the early years of the nineteenth century saw the beginning of the decline in the quality of the shows, and the one-time craze of society gradually slipped into temporary obliteration, by a graduated scale of downward steps via the fairground booth and the streets. But art *is* long, and family traditions die hard, and because of this, the Manning's and the Clunn Lewis's, the De Marion's, Delvaine's and D'Arc's, faithful to their art, did their shows in the same way as their fathers had done before them, and so kept alive this wonderful thing, the oldest entertainment in the world. To this very day the descendants of some of these people operate ancestral marionettes, dressed and re-dressed, painted and repainted a dozen times and more. Other troupes have gone out of existence and their dolls form much prized items in many collections. A list of some of these old-time showmen is given at the end of this book.

Some account of these bygone puppet masters is given in "Everybody's Theatre," and it would be but repetition to print it again in this present volume. At the same time, it might not be amiss to describe some of the *characters* and *acts* usually seen in one of these early performances. Of the very primitive shows only occasional details exist. A good deal of the spectacular side of the show seemed to consist of cut-out and painted tableaux, usually of a religious or historical nature. It is interesting to note that Robert Powell, most famous of all the eighteenth century puppet showmen, used to parade some of his dolls on horseback through the streets of Bath, where he showed, as well as at Oxford and London, by way of rounding up an audience. An excellent description of Powell's show is given in Chambers's "*Book of Days*," volume II, page 167. In the same volume, page 244, is given the details of a programme of an entertainment to be held at Mr. Punch's Theatre about the end of the seventeenth century. This theatre, it appears, was situated at the upper end of St. Martin's Lane, adjoining Litchfield Street.

It is of the nineteenth century showmen

Fig. 1.—Powell's Puppet Show.
Powell himself is portrayed in the foreground.

and their productions that the most detailed descriptions exist. William Hone in his "Everyday Book," page 1,114, tells of Candler's Fantoccini, which he saw performing in the streets of Pentonville, and George Cruikshank, who was with him at the time,

supplies a very carefully drawn illustration of the show. The date of the performance is given as August, 1825, and the details of the acts which follow, show the type of performance which became a tradition to be followed by nearly every puppet showman throughout the century. In Candler's show there appeared:—
1. A *tumbler* and posture master; 2. A *skeleton* which came to pieces; 3. A *clown* with extending neck; 4. A *polander* or pole balancer with chairs; 5. A *sailor* dancing a hornpipe; 6. An Indian *ball juggler*, and 7. *Billy Waters*, a wooden-legged fiddler.

Many years later Henry Mayhew in his "*London Labour and the London Poor*," gave a detailed description of a street fantoccini show in an interview with an actual showman of his day, about 1860, and it will be seen how many of the acts had become a tradition in the programme that this performer presented. *Dolls two feet high* :—1. *Female hornpipe dancer* ; 2. *Quadrille* of four female dancers; 3. *Mr. Grimaldi*, the clown, tumbler and comic dancer; 4. *The Enchanted Turk* who "threw off" arms and legs, which all became separate figures, two boys, two girls; the head, a clergyman; the body, an old lady; 5. *The Old Lady*, another separating figure, arms became two figures, body became a balloon and car. The figures get into the car and the balloon ascends; 6. *Tight-rope dancer* ; 7. *Indian ball juggler*

(Ramo Samee); 8. *Sailor* dancing a hornpipe; 9. *Polander* with chairs; 10. *Skeletons*; 11. *Judy Gallagher*, another separating figure; 12. *Countryman and obstinate donkey*;

Fig. 2.—1825. A Street Marionette Theatre, sketched by George Cruikshank and described by William Hone.

13. *Skeleton* which falls to pieces; 14. *Nondescript comic figure* which falls to bits and plays catchball with his head; 15. A *scene* from "Tom and Jerry"; 16. *Scotsman* who does

a Highland fling; 17. *Flower girl*, or Fairy Garland Dance.

A comparison of these two programmes will show the great similarity between the acts, and in the Rozella troupe, and again in a troupe known as "Archibald's Marionettes," both of the late Victorian era, and both now in the possession of the London Marionette Theatre, these very same acts occur, together with others of a more topical nature, illustrative of their own particular period. Practically all of the marionette shows of the nineteenth century had in their programmes dolls doing these acts, and many of the shows carried on to-day by the descendants of the great showmen exhibit these same traditional acts in exactly the same manner as they were shown when our great-great-grandparents were little children gazing with wondering eyes at a puppet show in a fair.

The *Enchanted Turk*, also known as the *Grand Turk*, was the *pièce de résistance* of the whole performance, and the figure belonging to the famous Barnard troupe of the old Royal Aquarium days stood five feet or more in height before it "disintegrated," a tremendous doll. In many cases the puppets were hideous affairs, crudely carved and roughly put together. In other troupes, the Barnard and the D'Arc for instance, the standard of quality was extremely high. The Barnard dolls, in particular, being very finely finished, and with well carved heads. Papier mâché was used in some cases, but most of the dolls were carved and ranged from two to three feet in height, in some cases almost life size.

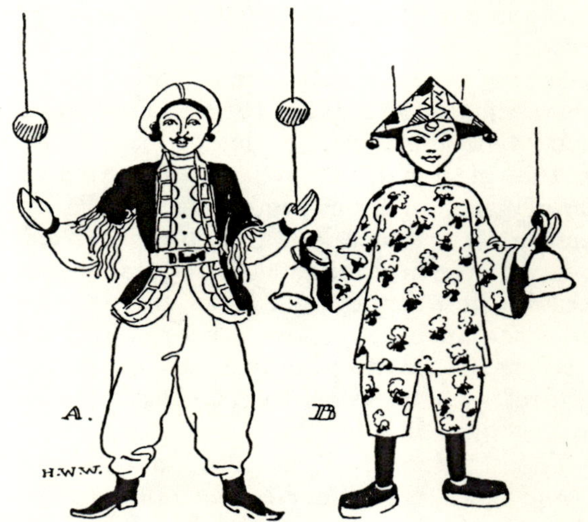

Fig. 3.—Traditional marionettes. (*a*) Ramo Samee (Archibald Troupe). A stock figure, evidently made for the trade. (*b*) One of the pair of Japanese Bell Dancers (Rozella).

All this meant a correspondingly big " fit-up." Seawood's marionettes had a stage twenty feet in width, and many other troupes had stages much larger than this, so that transport and portability became a very serious item in the business. There were no motor lorries and tractors in those days, and they were far too big affairs to be pushed around on a pair of wheels as the Punch men transported their shows.

Most of the showmen went in for a very heavy and elaborate proscenium, highly decorated in gaudy colours. They manipulated their dolls in front of great drop scenes, with wings and borders entirely in the manner of the "penny plain and tuppence coloured" theatres of their day. In the list which follows, some idea can be obtained of the shows which toured the country at the end of the eighteenth century and throughout the Victorian era. This list is by no means complete, nor can it ever be completed. Many of the troupes no longer exist, the "fit-up" and the dolls are destroyed, and no record has been left to remind posterity of their existence. Now and again someone digs out an old box of puppets, and the daylight reveals their faded, moth-eaten finery, their broken limbs and hopelessly tangled strings. When the writer and his partner purchased the Rozella dolls, the poor little actors were jumbled together into one great and inseparable tangle, so that all the strings of *all* the dolls had to be cut away before one could even examine them, to see what they were like. These puppets had been stored away for years, and there must be even now, marionettes that formed part of some of the greater troupes lying buried in places yet to be revealed, to say nothing of the dolls of more or less unknown showmen in a similar plight.

For, like all successful things, the great puppet showmen had their imitators. Some were amateurs who produced their little troupes from Dutch dolls and other obtainable figures, and who did the whole business merely to amuse themselves and their friends. Others were professionals whose lack of knowledge and art coupled, perhaps, with an inability to "put the show across," or showmanship, never got beyond a mediocrity which killed their efforts and banished the outfit into obscurity.

SOME OLD-TIME PUPPET SHOWS IN ENGLAND

1710.—Powell's Puppet Show. Powell was famous for his "Queen of Sheba" and "Garden of Eden."

1711.—Pinkethman.

1711.—Crawley. "The Old Creation" and "The Flood."

1737.—Charlotte Clarke's Puppet Show. The Tennis Court, James Street, near the Haymarket.

1737.—Russel's Puppets at Kickford's, Great Rome, Brewer Street.

1763.—Mr. Yates. The fantoccini in London.

1790.—Flocton's Puppet Show. Flocton boasted of five hundred dolls, all working.

Fig. 4.—The Grand Turk and his transformation.

17—? to 1800.—Henry Rowe represented Shakespeare's plays with puppets. He recited the whole of the drama himself. He was a native of York and worked in that area. In 1797 he published his puppet version of "Macbeth" with notes. He died in 1800.

1850-51.—At the ADELAIDE GALLERY. Little is known of this revival, but details and a picture were published in the *Illustrated London News* of the day. The troupe was fairly large and had an extensive repertoire.

1772.—THE ITALIAN FANTOCCINI at Panton Street, Haymarket.

1776.—Notice in the *Morning Post* of the day:

THE PATAGONIAN THEATRE, Exeter Change.

1778.—The same.

1779.—*Morning Post*, April 14th:

THE ITALIAN FANTOCCINI, at Panton Street, Haymarket. These marionettes were exhibited by Mr. Carlo Perrico. They did a play called "Harlequin, Great Sorcerer." Also a pantomime by the large family of the JEALOUS PIERROT, with additional "New Metamorphoses."

1818.—LAVERGE'S ROYAL GALLANTEE SHOW. Exhibited in Ely Court, Holborn Hill. He showed "The Passion of Jesus Christ," "Noah's Ark," "The Prodigal Son" and other tableaux.

1825.—CANDLER'S FANTOCCINI. Described by Hone in his "Everyday Book," and mentioned in an earlier part of this chapter.

GRAY'S FANTOCCINI. One of the first marionette shows to appear on the London streets. The actual date is unknown, but it was in the very early part of the nineteenth century that the Scotsman,

Fig. 5.—A fairy of the D'Arc Troupe and the famous "Mother Shipton" of the Clunn Lewis' Marionettes.

Gray, carried his troupe of nine-inch marionettes around the towns. Later he exhibited a show at Vauxhall Gardens with dolls about two feet in height. After Gray came MUMFORD'S DANCING DOLLS, and then MR. SEAWOOD'S MARIONETTES.

1828.—THE FRENCH THEATRE. "Du Petit Lazary des Messrs. Maffey de Paris." September 2nd, at the Argyll Rooms, Regent Street. The figures were two feet high. This may have been "Le Petit Theatre Matthiew" which performed Shakespeare's tragedies and farces at the Argyll Rooms. Their puppets were *modelled*, not carved, and their dolls "stood as high as a table;" they worked from a very high platform. They removed afterwards to the Western Institution, Leicester Square.

1830-40.—MR. BROWN'S PUPPET THEATRE, at the Royal Victoria Hall and Coffee Tavern, Waterloo Road.

"Every evening:—PROFESSOR WHATMAN'S INTERNATIONAL MARIONETTES." Professor Whatman did the regulation traditional show, with pole balancer, dissecting skeleton, Japanese bell dancers, comic donkey cart act and pantomime.

About 1880-81.—W. BULLOCK'S ROYAL MARIONETTES (from Liverpool), at Great St. James' Hall, Regent Street. The dolls had wooden limbs, with wax or papier mâché heads. They performed the usual fantoccini show and finished with a grand pantomime, "Little Red Riding Hood."

D'ARC'S WONDERFUL MARIONETTES.

One of the greatest troupes of marionettes that have been seen in the country. The dolls are now in the collection of H. H. Peach, Esq., of Leicester.

1887 ?—MARSHALL and HARTLEY.

1887 ?—ALLY SLOPER'S JUBILEE MARIONETTES.

1884.—CHESTER and LEE'S ROYAL MARIONETTES. A fine troupe with an established reputation and still performing.

1884.—At the Agricultural Hall. Christmas. In King Edward's Hall. THE SMALLEST AND MOST COMPLETE MARIONETTE THEATRE in the world. The proprietor's name is, so far, unknown, but the dolls were *three and a half inches* in height, they were " all made to work " and amongst the scenes were a " Drawing Room Set " and " Captain Webb and the Falls of Niagara," which all goes to show how the marionette man of the Victorian era missed no opportunities of keeping his show up-to-date.

At the Albert Palace, Battersea Park, in the Nave, MR. BRITTON PETTIGROVE exhibited his NEW GRAND NATIONAL MARIONETTES. In this entertainment the traditional acts were shown, there was " Mons. and *Mdme.* Blondin " on the tight rope. There was "Signor Tranca, the Spanish pole dancer," " Tommy and

Sally the London street singers," the inevitable "skeleton," the "Chinese Carnival"—probably our old friends the Japanese bell dancers, under a new guise, and also a grand pantomime, "Beauty and the Beast."

Barnard's Marionettes at the Royal Aquarium, Westminster. A very fine traditional troupe. The puppets were made by Mr. Barnard and are still in the possession of the family, who have operated them in all parts of the world. They formed the subject for a full page cartoon in *Punch* when a certain law case occurred in which Mr. Barnard scored a tremendous triumph.

Rozella's Marionettes. A traditional troupe. Very popular in the late nineteenth century. Performed at the Mansion House Children's Parties, and Society occasions. Puppets average fourteen inches in height.

Middelton Brothers' Royal and Original Marionettes. A famous Kentish troupe that later became the Clunn Lewis' Marionettes. One of the oldest existing troupes in the country. The doll known as "Mother Shipton," a very early type of "smoking" doll, is nearly three centuries old and, during the reign of Queen Anne, its hollow body was used by smugglers for bringing contraband lace into the country.

Holden's "Fantoches." A very famous troupe with a world-wide reputa-

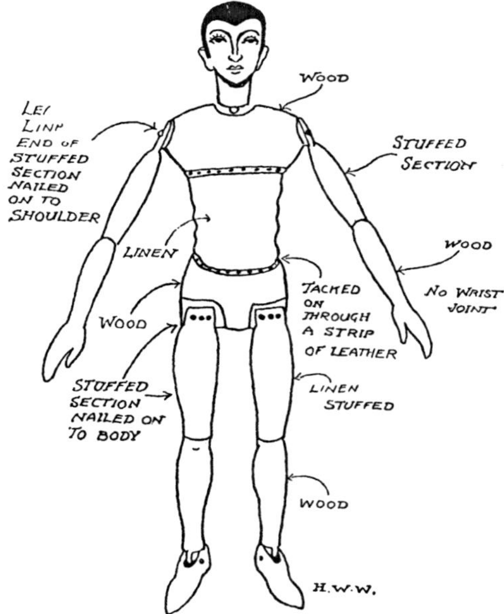

Fig. 6.—Constructional details of the old English traditional marionette.

tion like the D'Arc troupe. Has been in existence for many years, and the name holds good to-day as a first-class show of its kind.

BOLTON'S MARIONETTE PLAYS AND VARIETIES. A traditional troupe operating in the Yorkshire districts.

DE MARION'S ROYAL COURT MARIONETTES. HARRY FANNING. One of the most famous of the travelling shows of this country and, like many of the other great shows, with a very widely travelled history and a reputation that goes back for many, many years. Like other big troupes it is a family affair, ancestral one might say, in which succeeding generations are taught the art and attain a marvellous proficiency at manipulating at a very early age. Harry Fanning, the veteran proprietor of this stupendous show, built another well-known troupe of puppets, the clever

JESS JEWELL'S MARIONETTES. The author has an unforgettable memory of this troupe as the very first marionette performance he ever saw, and that was when as a schoolboy, he made their acquaintance at the "Victorian Era" Exhibition held at Earl's Court in 1897. Incidentally these were by no means the first marionettes to appear at that famous London pleasure resort, for in 1888, at the Italian Exhibition, the BROTHERS PRANDI of Brescia, exhibited their "celebrated marionettes" with the grand ballet

" Amor," and other dramatic and operatic productions.

Coupled with the name of De Marion is that of DELVAINE'S MARIONETTES. Another of the best known troupes in the country. Following the traditional lines in its programme this show has its own puppet orchestra and some very funny personages in the boxes on either side of the stage. The manipulation is extremely clever, particularly in some of the specialised " turns." The author had the pleasure of seeing these figures at the famous " Barnard's " Music Hall in Chatham—completely destroyed by fire in 1934—and judging by the reception they had, has no hesitation in describing them as a " tremendous success."

This list would be incomplete without the name of HARRY WILDING'S MARIONETTES, a troupe which made a great name for itself in the Midlands, and, at a later part of the book, mention will be found of other famous men who have brought this art to perfection in modern times.

CHAPTER II

PUPPETRY IN FOREIGN COUNTRIES

APART from the traditional programme there are also traditional styles and types of puppets, as well as methods of manipulation. This is exhibited more particularly on the Continent where the various European countries have each their own peculiar manner and mode of production. In France and Russia, for example, the national puppet is a sleeve doll, after the fashion of the English Punch and Judy. Belgium has its famous marionettes controlled from above by a single wire. In Cologne, Christopher Winter founded in 1802 a marionette theatre called the Hänneschen Theatre. In this theatre the puppets were controlled from below the stage, each supported on a wire which was fixed into a long pole like a broomstick, and this method of manipulation is used right up to the present time in the Hänneschen Theatre of Cologne. In Czechoslovakia the national marionette has a main wire into the head, and strings to control the movements of arms and legs, and a similar type of control is used on the Italian dolls, and those of Sicily.

Not only methods of manipulation have passed from generation to generation, but the characteristics of the dolls, the technique of construction, their costumes and, in many cases the *expression* on their faces has become a tradition, faithfully kept alive by a long succession of craftsmen handing down from

Fig. 7.—The Hanneschen Theatre of Cologne. Behind the scenes, showing method of manipulating, and two of the characters.

father to son the heirloom of a family art, the laws of which no scion of the race would ever dare to question, much less to consider the possibility of a change of style.

Examples of this traditional costume and type may be seen in the French puppet "Guignol," a character which was created by

Laurent Mourquet in the latter end of the eighteenth century, but is to-day still dressed in a tri-cornered hat, and wears a pigtail and coat of the period of his conception. "Tchantche," the beloved marionette of Liege, wears always the same broad grin across his block-like face, and is invariably dressed in the baggy, white trousers, blue smock and high-crowned black hat of the Walloon peasant, of the days when the great battles for liberty brought independence to the Belgian people. "Tchantche" has earned a distinction that no other puppet, and not even Mr. Punch, can claim, that is of having a statue in a public square in Liege erected to his name. There is also Mr. Punch, whose features never vary, whose character is always the same, whose costume smacks of Elizabethan days and whose baton and coxcomb headgear of an even earlier time.

Tradition has a tremendous influence also on the craftsmen who design and make many of the dolls. The Sicilian puppet makers and the men who carve the Belgian marionettes keep as near as possible to the style and manner of the work of their ancient forebears. The marionettes of Liege with their strong, stern faces, their elaborately carved and decorated armour, are invariably given a sort of nondescript, Romano-mediæval appearance, that reminds one of the gorgeous puppets one sees adorning the front of a great roundabout organ at a fair; incidentally, many of those organ figures come from the Continent, so there may be some sort of a connection between them and the marionettes, for a very similar type of carving and costume is displayed on the Sicilian puppets too.

Another curious mannerism that has come down through the years is that of making the important figures considerably *larger* than the lesser actors. In the "Tchantche" theatres Charlemagne and Roland are giants compared to the troops who fight in "la battaille," and to the courtiers who stand staring into space whilst the King makes a speech. Tchantche himself, the peasant, is only about half the size of his monarch.

These degrees of comparison, this suggesting of estate and quality by the height and immensity of the important people, and of the descent of the scale to the lower orders is as old as art itself. In all representations of early art the same thing can be found, the ancient Egyptian paintings show the same principle, with their gigantic Pharaohs and their hundreds of diminutive slaves. So it will be found to be universal in all Oriental puppets; in the wayangs of Java, the Burmese marionettes and the Chinese shadow figures. A primitive "Who's Who," a native "Debrett's," by which the audience can tell at a glance whether a character was a somebody or a nobody, a hero or a villain, a mortal or a god. There was another method of showing character besides making the figures tall or short, that was by enlarging the parts that represented the *nature* of the being. If he was a thief he had big hands, if he was inquisitive he had a big nose. If he was a god of war or some great,

Fig. 8.—Guignol, Tchantche and Punch. The figure of Punch is one of a complete set of street Punch and Judy figures—mid-Victorian—in the collection of E. Kersley, Esq.

evil spirit he was made as hideously ugly as the most virile imagination could devise; he would be successfully ugly, a nightmare of eyes, teeth and claws. If, on the other hand, he represented a god of goodness, a gentle creature loved by all and feared by none, then his every line suggested a benign and kindly spirit. His very attitude of quietude and peace was a definite contradiction to the roaring violence of the evil one.

In *The Bankside Book of Puppets* the author describes the Javanese and Chinese *shadow* figures. The Burmese *marionettes*, however, may have a place in this chapter because they are controlled by strings in much the same manner as other marionettes. Some of them have controls, the animals in particular, and the illustrations show some types of both classes. It will be seen that the strings of the man are continuous, that is, they start from one point, the hands for instance, and finish at the opposite point on the figure, from hand to hand, knee to knee, ear to ear, and so on. They would be held on the hand and wrist, and various attitudes could be made by simple movements of the arm and hand. The other hand being used for making specially important moves with the hands or feet. The animals are very successful, being capable of a great number of movements and attitudes. The wood used is extremely light in weight, and in appearance is something like the balsa wood of South America, so it follows that the dolls are not very strong affairs, and the joints are likely to come apart very easily. In India and China too there are stringed puppets, performed by strolling players in the majority of cases, who pass from village to town, erect a flimsy bamboo framework fit-up, lay a strip of carpet on the ground, and lo, a theatre has appeared.

Of all traditional European marionettes the Sicilian puppets are the most famous. Henry Festing Jones in his books, "Sicilian Diversions" and "Castellanaria and other Sicilian Diversions," gives graphic and detailed descriptions of the workings of Sicilian marionette theatres. The dolls are controlled by a main wire to the head and have a wire to their right wrist. In addition to these rods, a string goes to the left hand and additional strings are added for special movements. Some of the Sicilian dolls are almost life size, others about half life size, and each puppet is a full-time job for one operator. It is interesting to note that a certain "Grand Turk" occurs in these Sicilian puppet dramas, and one is tempted to wonder if there is any connection between this Sicilian notability and the Grand Turk the old English marionette showmen regarded as the "big hit" of their shows.

The descriptions given by Mr. Festing Jones of these Sicilian puppet shows could be used almost word for word in describing a puppet show in the Belgian town of Liege. The author having been privileged to witness one of these Belgian performances was struck by this similarity. The scenery, the puppets, the methods of manipulation, the action of the play, and last but not least, the actions of the audience, all tallied exactly with the performances at Liege, even to the eating of nuts during the waits.

In another great home of the puppets,

Fig. 9.—Burmese marionettes. A beggar and horse.

Germany, every type of doll may be found, from ancient sleeve dolls to ultra-modern marionettes. "Papa Smidt's" famous Marionette Theatre at Munich, Ivo Puhonny at Baden Baden, Paul Brünn at Munich, and Harro Seigel of Berlin, are but a few of the many efforts that have been, and are still being made, to advance this wonderful art and keep its traditions alive. The methods of manipulation-vary, but in the main, the fully stringed marionette without wires is used.

In Austria, Professor Richard Teschner has his exquisite theatre of the Magic Mirror at Vienna. His puppets, unlike any other dolls ever made in their delicate charm and marvellous grace, are operated from *below* the stage level by means of rods and tubes. The whole production being based on the Javanese wayangs, of which Professor Teschner has a personal and intimate knowledge. In Saltzburg, Professor Aicher runs an extremely well-equipped theatre with a fine collection of stringed marionettes and a most extensive repertoire.

To the British public the best known Continental troupe is the world famous " Teatro dei Piccoli " of Dr. Vittorio Podrecca. The headquarters of this theatre is in Rome, but its reputation is universal. A very noticeable feature of the performances by this troupe, is the speed in which most elaborate scenes are changed and the non-stop nature of the whole show which keeps the attention of the audience always centered on the stage. There are practically no waits and after all, this is a great achievement and tells of a perfect organisation at the back of the stage.

Other great Italian troupes are the Gorno

and Santoro troupes. The Gorno's came to England with Dr. Podrecca on his first visit, and remained in the country doing performances for several years, and are mentioned again in a later part of this book in the chapter dealing with the films.

In the New World puppetry is comparatively young, particularly as regards stringed marionettes. In the United States, Paul McPharlin, Garret Becker, James Juvenal Hayes, Tony Sarg, and the Yale Puppeteers are the outstanding names, to say nothing of Helen Hayman Joseph, the great authoress of a great book on the subject as well as a marionette producer of considerable note. Puppetry in the States is having a tremendous lift-up, it is increasing in popularity by giant strides, and real experimental work is being done on the dramatic side and on the technical side as well. Glove puppets and marionettes are the main mediums for the expression of the art, but Meyer Levin and other workers are producing plays in the coloured Chinese shadows, by which most delicately beautiful effects and movements can be obtained—the method of producing these shadows is fully described in *The Bankside Book of Puppets.*

So it seems that the whole world is becoming puppet minded, and a very good thing it will be for the world when it does realise what a beautiful thing is locked up in this art. Though, even to-day, the average person hardly knows what a puppet is; in almost every performance one gives, there are persons who tell you that they have seen marionettes for the first time, never knew they existed before. Which means that a good deal of spade work remains yet to

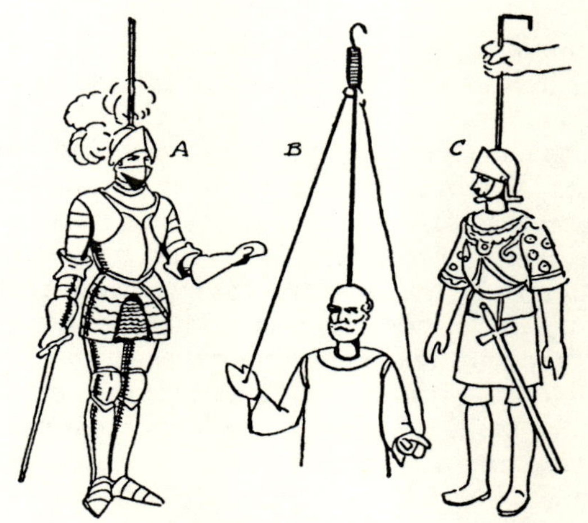

Fig. 10.—(*a and b*) Sicilian marionettes. (*c*) Belgian.

be done before the "house-full" boards become a nightly practice. But the big thing about it all is the international spirit that exists and grows stronger as the years go by. The friendly, helpful relations between British, German, French, Austrian, and all the other nations in this marionette art, a sort of spiritual freemasonry by which we are linked together like a silver chain around the world, the universal brotherhood of art. As a means towards making this brotherhood an accomplished fact, and a definite reality, the international society of *Unima* was formed. It

Fig. 11.—Marionettes of the great Italian, Teatro dei Piccoli.

began in Czechoslovakia a few years ago, and although, for the most part, its members are Continental, it has a world-wide reach, and has been the means of linking up the puppet workers of many lands. Dr. Jindrich Vesely, of Prague, was first president and retains that position to this day of writing.

Before passing on to the actual business, the practical side of the book, it will be a fitting close to this chapter if mention is made to what, in the author's opinion, is a group of the most wonderful puppets ever made, this is the series of characters made by the Czecho-slovakian producer, Dr. Joseph Skupa, and it consists of the marionette " Špejbl " and the small boy " Hurvineck," his sister and a dog. These marionettes are the star turns of the " Theatre Artistique de Pilsen." They are just caricatures in human form, but as marionettes they are the last word in perfection, they "think; " Spejbl, who incidentally, is duplicated and triplicated, is a masterpiece of characterisation. He is the father of Hurvineck, and sometimes he has him on his knee and tries to answer the strange questions the little boy, like " leedle Yawcoub Strauss," fires off at his father. Sometimes he winds a gramophone and sets it going as an accompaniment to Hurvineck's solo on a xylophone. Whatever it is, the thing is so real, so human, that it can send the whole of an international audience, not one fifth of which understand a single word of the conversation, into tears of laughter and shrieks of absolute joy, and that, for a marionette, is success.

CHAPTER III

THE STAGE

ONE cannot do much without a stage, but some people can do a great deal with a very simple one. In India and China as already mentioned and, no doubt, other Oriental countries, the itinerant puppet showmen carry around a few bamboo poles and three or four strips of coloured cloth and with these produce a most excellent portable theatre; usually with a cloth laid on the ground itself as a stage floor.

This same idea should be the guiding star of the puppet stage builder in this country if he contemplates travelling about from place to place with his fit-up.

If, however, the intention is to build a *permanent* theatre in a hall or studio, the boot is on the other foot, for though the main principles of construction will be the same, the details and materials employed will be quite different.

Actually, the marionette stage is a miniature replica of that of a real theatre, in that it consists of a proscenium, a stage floor, scenery and arrangements for lighting. But there is this about a marionette stage that will not be seen in any real theatre—the "bridge." If the theatre is for very large marionettes this bridge will be just exactly what its name suggests; if, however, the producer uses smaller figures, the bridge will be but a strong frame at the back of the stage area which supports the weight of

Fig. 12.—Two types of bridge for operating.

the operators leaning over it, and the back drop scenes—if any—at the same time. Illustrated in Figure 12 are two types of bridges. One being of the larger type and one being of the smaller in the form of a cyclorama or sky back cloth suitable for use with cut scenes and standing units.*

In the case of a permanent theatre, the structure must be adapted to the size and shape of the hall or room in which it is to be built, and a very necessary feature will be the allowance of as much room as possible back stage, in order that the operator's assistants may have free access to the principals when changing and replacing dolls during a performance. If the back stage area is cramped there may be many unwanted and unexpected things happen while a show is on, to cause delays—and delays are fatal.

The most important points to be borne in mind when building the stage are its *strength* and *rigidity*. It *must be strongly built* because, not only will it have to support a number of operators, as well as a lot of other fittings, and possibly a radio gramophone at the back, but also it must be strong enough for all these people to *move about*, change places one with another, and get up and down and on and off when necessary.

Hence the rigidity as well as the strength, for without these important factors the stage might as well be chopped up for firewood. Nothing would spoil a show more than for the audience to see a series of paralytic wobbles take place at intervals, as though the whole

* *See The Bankside Book of Puppets*, Chapter X.

structure was overcome by an attack of "nerves."

This means that in the case of a fixed stage a very strong *undercarriage* must be constructed with stout " four by two " uprights to support the floor boards. The floor boards themselves being of " one inch " planking with

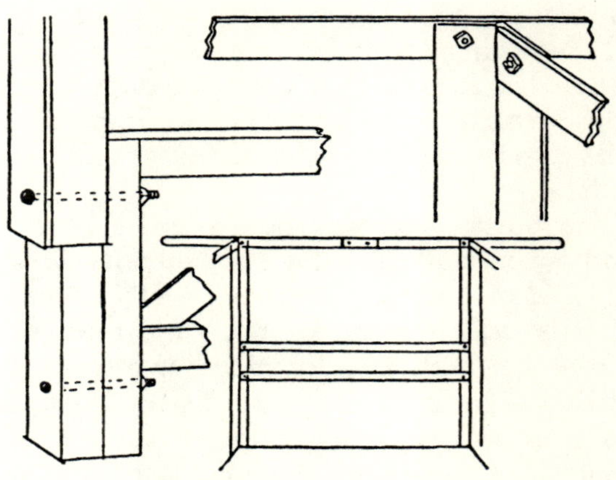

Fig. 13.—The travelling stage. Methods of assembling.

a removable section in the centre of the acting area for understage lighting effects and other tricks, *Figure* 13.

If the producer-to-be is but an indifferent carpenter it will be by far the best plan to call in the services of an experienced and practical woodworker, as it is essential that not only the undercarriage but every other detail of the structure be carefully and properly made.

The *proscenium* should be built from floor to ceiling, cutting off completely the auditorium from the stage, and allowing no light whatever to come from behind it during any part of a show, so that the audience see a complete,

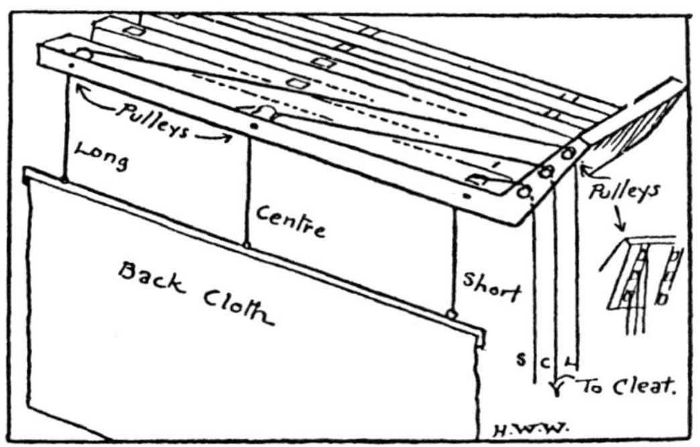

Fig. 14.—The grid system for flying scenery.

solid, black wall before them, broken only by the stage opening when the curtain rises on the play. The frame of the proscenium must be of stout wood, the panelling, however, can be of three-ply wood or beaver board. If there is room, have a door on either side of the proscenium.

If the hall or room has an exceptionally

high ceiling the back cloths and other scenic details can be " flown "; that is a " grid iron," a framework with a series of pulley wheels on which the ropes will run, can be suspended—fixed is the better word—high above the stage and the scenes raised and lowered into position as required. Before this is done, however, it would be well for the producer and carpenter too, to get a look at the " grid " and back stage of a real theatre. *Figure* 14 gives in a simple way a general idea as to how the " grid " system is operated.

The *Bridge* in a theatre of this type should be well above the stage, the floor level, four feet or more, according to the height of the marionettes to be used. For dolls twenty inches to two feet in height the bridge should be at least four feet, and so on. This will mean that fairly long strings or " slangs " will be used, but a bridge of this type, especially if it can be a separate item, not fixed to the stage, and on runners to allow a forward or backward movement, will be found extremely useful for a great variety of effects and give the producer a chance to use a deep or shallow stage according to the requirements of the play.

The *Proscenium Opening* will be affected also by the height of the dolls. For eighteen- to twenty-inch puppets it should be from five to seven feet in width and about two feet six inches in height. For twenty-four-inch dolls,

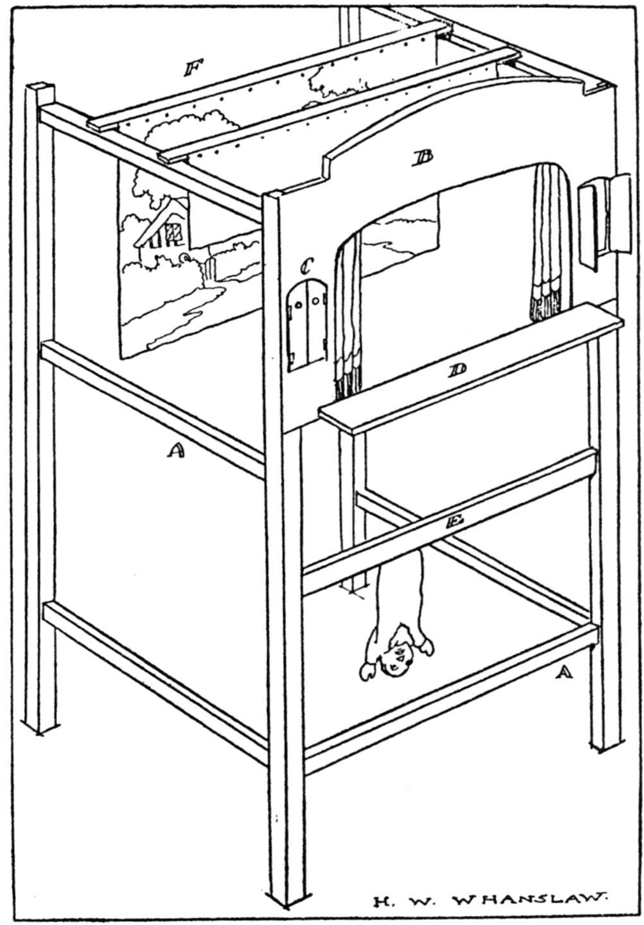

Fig. 15.—Main details of travelling fit-up.

six to eight feet wide and about three feet high, and for three-foot puppets at least nine feet wide and four feet in height.

All this means that the larger the dolls the bigger the stage, the scenery, the properties, everything in fact, and in consequence, increase of *weight* in all details. A " three-foot " doll, for instance, if made almost entirely of wood will be a very hefty affair to handle, and a great " pull " on the operator's arms, especially if it has to be " on " for any length of time. All this is worth consideration before one starts to build, and it will be just as well for the would-be producer to think of the stuff his assistants will have to handle, before coming to a decision as to the size of the outfit he intends to make.

The *depth* of the stage, if a sliding bridge is used, can be varied to suit the different needs of a production, but if the bridge is a fixture the stage should be about three to four feet in depth, so that an operator can lean over and make alterations to lights or turn the pages of the manuscript on the reading desk without any undue effort.

The *height* of the stage above the floor level of the hall will be governed to a certain extent by the seating arrangements in the auditorium. If there is a definite rake in the auditorium, the rows of seats rising in tiers from the front to the back of the hall, the stage floor need not be so high as when the hall floor is on a dead level. The builder will have to use his own judgment in a case of this description, certain experiments with temporary openings being tried out in order to decide on the right stage level for every one in the audience to see the feet as well as the heads of the puppets. If the stage is too high the front row of stall holders will not see the bottom half of the dolls, and if it is too low the "gallery" will not see the heads.

On a level floor the stage can be about four feet in height, but if the hall is very large this height must be increased, and here again the view-point tests can be carried out to advantage.

THE *TRAVELLING "FIT-UP*." The type chosen for this book is one that has been used by the London Marionette Theatre for many hundreds of performances in all parts of England and Wales. It can be erected quite easily and quickly, and for a big portable stage it packs into a comparatively small compass. It was designed by W. S. Lanchester, and the actual fit-up used by the London Marionette Theatre has had a severe testing, in that it has been built up in all kinds of situations, in theatres, shops, halls and schoolrooms, in corners and in many awkward and difficult places. This portable theatre has stood securely and rigid with sometimes as many as five operators and assistants upon it.*

The main details of construction are shown in *Figure* 15. There are four rectangular corner uprights which bolt into the four ends of the undercarriage. These uprights are held in position by four top bars, the front top bar being in two sections and longer by two feet or more on either side of the front uprights. Another frame bolts on to the front and carries the arrangements for the act curtains and the reflectors and lamps for the light.

The stage floor consists of three sets of "one-inch" planking and each section dovetails into its neighbour. The whole structure is *seven* feet wide and deep—a square—and *ten* feet in height from ground to top bars.

The proscenium consists of thick furnishing velvet curtains, deep green in this particular case. Everything is perfectly plain, no decoration or ornamentation whatever being employed, and the act curtains are of the same material as those which form the proscenium. This type of theatre and draped front was recommended by the author in an earlier book†, and from practical experience it has been

* A special Blue Print with full details of the stage, and published by the London Marionette Theatre.

† "Everybody's Theatre," H. W. Whanslaw. Wells Gardner, Darton & Co., Ltd.

found to be the ideal stage for travelling purposes, and it will be seen that if the drapery proscenium is done in a rich brown, or grey, or green the theatre will be in artistic harmony with the decorative schemes of the majority of places into which it is erected. For this purpose it will be well to avoid all forms of

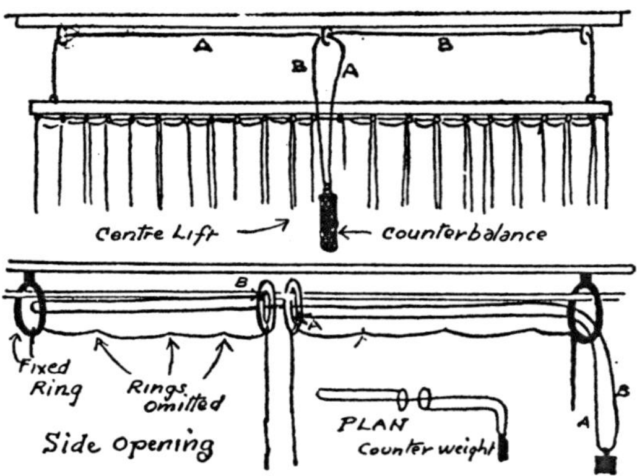

Fig. 16.—Two types of curtain fittings.

decoration in order that there may be nothing to clash with the decorative scheme of the hall itself.

Rods with removable hooks are used for the proscenium curtains and others can be suspended across inside the theatre on which the dolls can be hung when not in use, *Figure* 16. Also it will be well to fit a pair of

" gallows " of the same kind as described in *The Bankside Book of Puppets*. These gallows will be found particularly handy for use in dramatic productions, as well as for photographic purposes, in holding the puppets in position while pictures are being taken.

All kinds of hooks and " gadgets " will be found useful, but care must be taken to put odd fittings of this description in places where they will not interfere in any way with the entries or exits of the puppets.

The *Act Curtains* should be of *light-proof* velvet, which means that if they are made of the same material as the proscenium hangings they may have to be *lined*. This is to prevent leakage of light through to the audience whilst a scene is being set, and shadows or impressions of the movements on the stage being seen. The method of fitting up this curtain is illustrated in *Figure* 16. This curtain opens sideways from the centre, as it will be found that on the portable stage it is a rather difficult matter to make a lift-up curtain, the method employed is shown in *Figure* 16, but it will be seen that for a curtain of this description an absolutely clear run up and down is necessary. The side opening curtain has a special advantage in that it can be opened full width or only for a very small part, allowing the use of an announcing figure to appear before a black drop even while a main scene is set, also smaller scenes can be set before larger ones for time saving purposes.

In a real theatre the stage has a very definite "rake." It is lower in the front than at the back, but on a marionette stage such a rake is quite unnecessary, for one reason that the

Fig. 17.—Back-scene bridge and sliding wings with a standing unit in front of back scene.

acting area is very shallow, and for another reason that the standing units of scenery and properties will retain their positions better on a level surface, and also the dolls themselves require a perfect level for their movements around.

The *Bridge* for the portable theatre can be made a part of the back scene. It can be built on a strong framework and faced with three-ply, or even in the form of a shallow box, so that the top becomes the rest and the two plywood sides can be painted as different scenes for reversing. The side wings are screens securely held by a base board and they can be placed in various positions on the stage according to the producer's requirements. *Figure* 17 illustrates this back scene bridge and the side screens. It will be absolutely necessary to fix the bridge very firmly to the stage in order that it may not topple over when an operator leans rather heavily against it. The side screens will be found particularly useful as " bays," into which an operator may stand and so work from the side of the scene. This is the type of bridge and scene used by the London Marionette Theatre and it proved to be extremely reliable. With a fixed back bridge and the side screens movable, one could get at the stage with ease and this made for speed in the re-arrangement or changing of scenes and especially for the setting of properties on the stage.

If the play is to be a " set " affair, likely to be on for a run of performances and requiring but little or no great scenic changes, the side screens can be fixed to the floor in the same manner as the bridge back. A good plan is to bolt the side screens through the stage floor by means of a bolt and fly nut (*Figure* 13). With this arrangement the wings can be turned at various angles. In the place of screen wings flat frame wings may be used, with a long slot in their bases to allow them to be moved forwards on to the stage and back again, to act as maskings, for preventing the members of the audience who are sitting to the extreme right or left of the stalls from seeing through to the back of the stage to the puppets waiting their cue or coming into position for an entry, *Figure* 18.

As an additional means of strengthening the folding wing scenes when screwed to their base boards, iron brackets may be used as illustrated. It is obvious that these brackets must be strong, but not elaborate or big, so that the operator will not be stubbing the toes of his shoes against them while at work. Brackets like this will be required also to fix the bridge back-piece to its base.

The *Cyclorama Bridge*, described in *The Bankside Book of Puppets* will be found very useful for a large show, but it has its limitations in that, being a completely built structure it is not easy to pack and transport, and being curved it takes up a lot more room in a van than can be spared. The great thing for a travelling fit-up is to make everything as flat as possible, and the more the fittings fold up or take to pieces, the less space they will occupy when packed.

Before any definite step is made either in the purchase of materials or the construction of parts, it will be necessary to consider the all-important question of fire-proofing. For all public exhibitions and performances it is absolutely essential that materials used in the

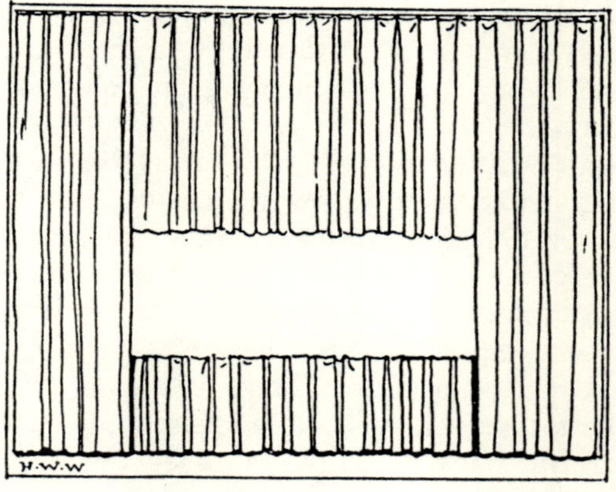

Fig. 18.—Curtain proscenium for a travelling fit-up.

outfit, stage, scenery, properties, etc., should be made fire-proof in order to comply with the law regarding the safety of human life. There are various fire-proofing solutions that can be purchased with which the details can be treated and it is possible also to get "fireproofed " wood of every kind and beaver board material for the curtains and other details. All of these materials can be used without fear of an inspector condemning the show as unfit for a public hall. It means that the original cost of materials will be increased to a certain extent, but this increase is not a very substantial matter in comparison to the fact that, in taking care to be on the right side of the law, the possibility of unpleasant complications in this direction is entirely removed.

" Safety First " applies to the proprietor of the outfit as well as to his assistants and his audience. It will be well for the person who is responsible for the whole production to look into this matter of public safety very carefully before going too far with the business, and there are various societies which will willingly give him advice and assistance.

It may be that his show is but a very small affair, but when there is even the slightest possibility of coming into danger, whether it be by fire or by electrical shocks, or by an unexpected accident—and who knows when an accident is *not* likely to occur ? Though that possibility seems to be very small and far away, it is a wise plan to be ready for the emergency. Prompt action can often avoid a calamity, and a knowledge is recommended of the various *rules* and *regulations* issued by the Board of Trade and the Home Office, also the rules issued by the Institution of Electrical Engineers, which have to be complied with before any fire insurance offices and other authorities will agree to issue a policy or to connect up an installation.

In passing, a description of some of the directions used in the real theatre may be found useful for the producer when the stage is ready to be used:

" R." means " right." The *actor's* right-hand *not* the right of the audience.

" L." means " left " on the same principle.

" Up Stage." Towards the back of the stage.

" Down Stage." Coming towards the footlights.

" Masking." When a figure stands in front of another important character and prevents the audience from seeing it clearly.

" 1st Entrances." Those nearest the audience.

" 2nd Entrances." Those nearer the back, " up stage."

CHAPTER IV

SCENERY AND PROPERTIES

LIKE the stage and fit-up, the scenery for a travelling theatre *must be portable*. If the theatre is a permanently fixed affair, built sets and elaborate " props " can be used, but, when it comes to travelling and the matter of portability occurs, *then* the producer will have to consider such things as space and packing as well as weight. On a mobile stage, unless the properties and built pieces are very strongly made, they are likely to be knocked to bits in a very short while owing to their difficulty in being packed.

So that " simplicity " is a good watchword for the producer to bear always in mind when considering the scenic details required for a production. Plain back cloths on rollers are as useful as anything, and sets of black or grey curtain " tabs " that can be run across on a rod at any moment, and to which can be added a standing unit if required.

The *back cloths* can be painted to represent scenes in much the same manner as those on the real stage, but the author gives the same advice here as in all of his other books on this subject, keep the design simple, let it be done in *flat* masses of *bright* colour, with very little shading and, sometimes, a definite outline. Look at the scene you are painting from as far away as you can get, remembering the gallery's point of view. Let your trees be well drawn as regards *outline* and *shape*, but painted in

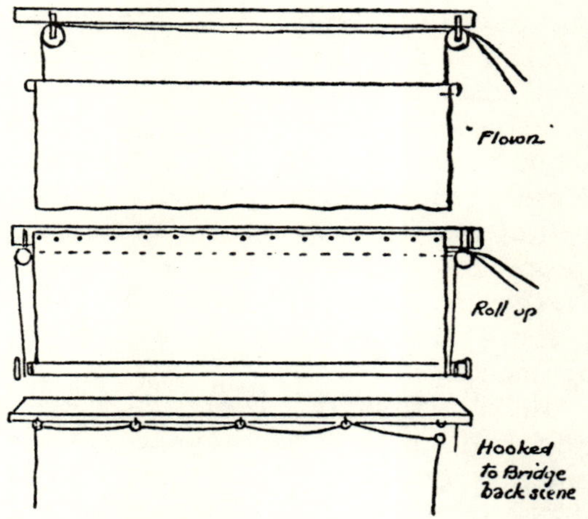

Fig. 19.—Methods of hanging back cloths.

broad masses of bright and sunny green. Distant foliage can be pale grey, and the foreground details in definite colour. Tree shadows, if any, can be in a faintly purplish blue, *not* a greenish blue, as the sense of shadow will be lost under artificial light.

The main colours of a theatrical scene painter's palette are:

White.
Lemon and orange chrome.
Light and dark ochre.
Raw sienna and burnt sienna.
Vandyke brown.
Venetian red and red lead.
Ultramarine blue and verditer blue.
Emerald green.
Indigo and drop black.

These colours are purchased in powder form and kept damp to prevent hardening. They are mixed with size which has been reduced by the addition of four pints of water to one pint of size. The material for the scene, if it is to roll up, should be either canvas or unbleached calico, and before the actual scene is painted on, this cloth is prepared by a surface painting of whitening and size.

Whatever the scene may be that is to be drawn, be sure to keep the horizon line low. A great fault with a number of scene painters is that they fix their horizon much too high up on the scene. This gives the effect, in a street scene for instance, of the main street, which is supposed to be a part of the stage itself, suddenly rising up like a hill in the background. Also, it makes the perspective of all the buildings entirely out of keeping with the dolls on the stage. The horizon line should be about the same level as the eyes of the dolls on the stage, no higher and, if anything, a trifle lower.

Figure 19 shows a drop back cloth with weighted base. Some producers prefer to hang their back scenes on hooks arranged along the lower front of the bridge, either by rings on the scene (*Figure* 19), or by simply resting the top rod of the scene upon hooks provided for that purpose. This is by far the best

Fig. 20.—Built scenery. Opening doors and windows for puppet exits and entrances.

method and makes for greater quickness in the changing of the scene. All kinds of methods are devised and suggested for this changing of scene.

If the bridge is of the box type already mentioned, the plywood face should be painted pale greenish blue and will serve as a sky scene, in front of which units and details can be set, *Figure* 20.

In the old days, all the effects of morning, evening, cloudy and stormy skies were painted directly on to the scene. To-day most of those effects are obtained by means of lighting and the use of colour screens—which is dealt with more particularly in the chapter on lighting. So that a simple, cloudless sky is all that is required, and if this is painted as described above, just a very pale blue in colour, all the atmospheric effects will be obtained quite easily on it.

Built scenes should be avoided as much as possible, and if the producer is using screen wings, interior effects can be obtained by a back scene with a cut window and the two screens for walls, *Figure* 20. Fireplaces, cupboards, etc., can be in the form of properties and placed into position against the screens. Too elaborate scenery will make the business complicated and, after all, much can be done by suggestion and effect, so that the simplest means of obtaining that effect should be the method that the producer will use.

The first thing that the manipulator will discover about his interior scenes is that it is impossible to make a stringed puppet enter or exit through an ordinary door in a wall. In the majority of cases the dolls make their entries through a space between the wings and

Fig. 21.—Scene designs.
For puppet exits and entrances.

back cloth, or in front of the wing screens. But there are some special occasions in which it is absolutely necessary for a puppet to enter by means of a window, or through a doorway. To do this the window will have to open casement-wise and pass right up to the top of the scene, that is, there will be no top of the window visible to the audience (*Figure* 20), and the same applies to a door, which must be built on to a panel so that the door and wall immediately above it will be hinged, and open in one piece, to allow the marionette strings to pass through. All this means that the scenery must be *too high* for the audience to see the top of it, or the proscenium opening is made proportionately low for the same reason. The producer will soon learn to work out schemes of this description to suit his plays, but one important point must be borne in mind at *all times*, and that is to make sure that all corners and ends of scenery are *well rounded off*, and free from small projections, or likely places where a string can catch on to during any entry. Nothing can spoil the appearance of a scene more than for the audience to see a clever entry of a doll spoiled by that same figure pulling up short, and suddenly lurching backwards, followed by frantic movements, indicating the fact that the operator is trying to clear a caught-up string. Therefore the person who makes the scenery will have to make perfectly sure that, as far as he is concerned, there is nothing about his work to cause such a calamity. This advice applies to all parts of the stage as well as to the entries, because, an odd drawing pin stuck into some part of the fit-up, or a hook wrongly placed, *anything*, may catch up a string, and it is surprising how such an apparently trivial thing

Fig. 22.—Properties mounted on a base.

as this can be the means of causing so great an amount of confusion.

During the action of a show, all scenery that is not to be used during the performance must be kept right out of the way. One assistant must be given the task of handling the scenery and properties, and his duty is to see that each set is ready to go "on" immediately the curtain falls on its predecessor. While an act is in progress he is getting the set ready for the next, and as soon as the act finishes he will clear the stage and reset the scene, *then* he will stack the used details in a place where they will not interfere with the rest of the performance. This means that sets to go " on " will have one place, and sets that are finished with, an entirely different place at the back of the stage, in order to prevent confusion and loss of time.

In *The Bankside Book of Puppets* mention is made of perspective and pictorial composition. Both of these arts should be studied by the scene designer in order that his scenes may appear reasonably accurate from the viewpoint of the audience.

Another aspect of the art to which a good deal of attention can be given is that of *symbolism*, wherein the scenes themselves may have a great part in the suggestive atmosphere of the play. A street of ancient houses lurching forward, almost toppling over, meeting their opposite neighbours at the top, gloomy and decrepit, can suggest foreboding and future evil. Anything dark and shadowy will give a hint of evil, but the leaning forward of things, like a high wall, adds a final touch to the scene, *Figure* 21. As a contrast to this, a wide open landscape with rolling, gentle hills, and tall poplar trees, standing straight, unswept by wind, gives a feeling of peace and rest, where again, a woodland scene of tangled trees and twisted boughs, with a deep and dark background into which no light occurs, suggests some fantastic forest peopled only by strange creatures of imagination.

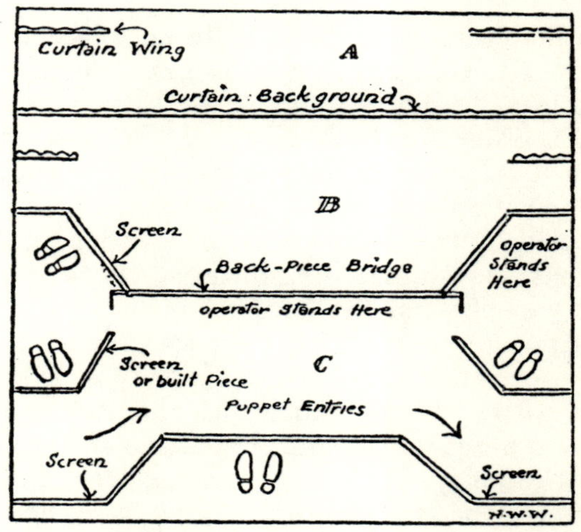

Fig. 23.—Stage plans of settings. (*a*) Straight curtain set. (*b and c*) Built up sets for depth. All are shown as from the operator's point of view.

A light, bright scene, full of colour and warmth, suggests happiness and comedy. A dark setting, full of heavy, purple shadows, against a deep blue, or green light, will give an immediate impression of sadness and impending tragedy.

The student is advised to make a special study of this important branch of the art. The works of great theatrical producers, masters of their art like Gordon Craig and Reinhardt, and outstanding films, too, can

Fig. 24.—A setting without scene or proscenium.

give a great deal of help towards an understanding of this section of the work. At the time of writing there is, on some of the London cinemas, a Japanese film entitled "Little Geisha Girl." In this picture the growth of a little child is symbolised, by the effect of the changing seasons on a single cherry tree, no human beings in the picture at all. There is the baby girl, then the cherry tree and its phases, after this the young girl turning into womanhood. An effect like this can be obtained on any stage by careful adjustment of the colours on the back scene to those of the lighting system.

A great deal of suggestive production can be done without the use of any scenery at all, simply by means of lighting and the black or grey tableau curtains. For this, however, a good spot-light is required. There are experimental puppeteers who go so far as to dispense with a proscenium and fit-up; stretch a black curtain across about five feet in height from the ground, set a spot-light on to the centre of the stage and, in a room in which this " spot " is the only light, they lean over the top of the curtain and perform their play. This is simplicity itself, and as the only light is that which centres on the dolls themselves, the audience is unable to see the operators above the curtain who, when the house lights are on, would be in full view.

So that the producer has a wide field open to him for his scenic effects. He can go from one extreme to the other. He can have detailed scenes with painted back cloths and carefully modelled properties, or he can have nothing at all save a curtain and a light.

Properties must be strongly made and, in

any special scene where a lot of small details are to be used, it will be an excellent plan to *fix* them on to a base board. Chairs, table and so on, when grouped together, will then be not only securely fixed without fear of being knocked over by a doll, but the whole " piece " can be picked up and shifted with the greatest ease and in the smallest amount of time.

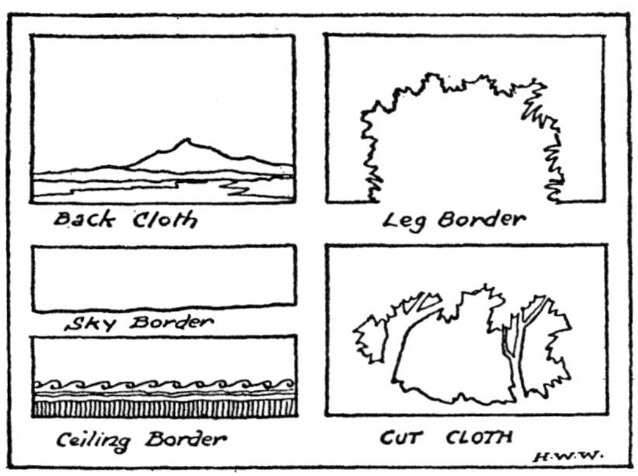

Fig. 25.—Types of stage " cloths."

Figure 22 illustrates a scene from " The Forest Fairy," in which this principle is used ; the main block of properties being a " one piece " affair. *All* properties must be made to stand solid and squarely on all corners, and not likely to rock about when a character passes near them. Too many pieces are to be avoided, and details made of china or glass or any other fragile substance, should also be " black listed " and debarred from being used, because of the possible danger of their breaking during transport as well as the difficulty in fixing them on to sets. Little wooden plates, pots, bowls and things of this description that can be glued or screwed down to tables or on shelves are useful details, but, whatever these items may be, it must always be borne in mind that they must be placed in such positions that the possibility of strings catching into them is entirely eliminated.

CHAPTER V

LIGHTING

THE old-time showmen used candles and oil lamps to illuminate their stage, a highly dangerous procedure at the best of times, and more than one fatal accident occurred as a result of this system. Rozella, for example, had triangular shaped trays in which he stood his footlight candles, and a couple of oil lamps that fitted into holders, on either side of his stage.

Electricity has altered all this to-day and, to a very great extent, removed the possibility of danger by fire, to say nothing of the tremendous improvement in the illumination of the scene.

In a real theatre there are " battens " and " floats," " spot-lights " and " pilot-lights," and in a permanent marionette theatre the same lighting system may be used, with one very important modification. There must be *no* overhead battens crossing the stage from side to side in any part of the acting area, or over any part of the stage where they are likely to interfere with the free entry or exit of the marionettes.

Therefore, the best system to adopt is that indicated in *Figure* 26, which shows ground, or side lights on either side of the proscenium and a row of lights, directly above the opening, which illuminate the back cloth as well as, to a certain extent, the acting area. The great thing to aim at in lighting a puppet stage is to so arrange the lamps that no bad shadows of the dolls are thrown upon the back scene.

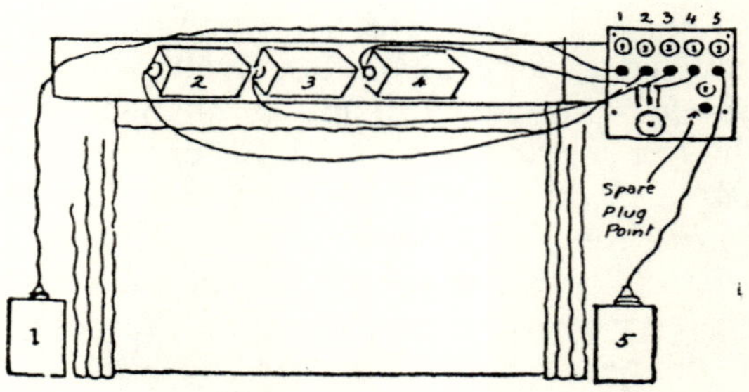

Fig. 26.—Simple lighting arrangement for the travelling stage.

Additional lights in the form of " spots " or pilot-lights—the latter are movable lamps on weighted pedestals, *Figure* 27—will be found to be extremely useful. A box-light on a long flex that can be used for understage effects, a " strip-light " for illuminating the sky from the stage level for sunrise and sunset effects. Various other uses of mobile lights will occur as the producer designs fresh arrangements for new scenes.

All the lights should be " boxed " in metal cases with polished reflectors, fitted with a groove around the front, or slot, into which colour screens can be placed. These slots must allow freedom of movement for the screens in order that quick changes of colour may be made without a hitch. They should be wide enough also, for two screens to be used at the same time, as sometimes a special slow change of colour can be effected by the passing out of one screen during the entry of another.

For a portable theatre, the most practicable system of lighting is illustrated in *Figure* 26. A pair of mobile side lights, if powerful enough, will be sufficient to light a " five-foot " stage for travelling use, but, if the producer wishes to put on more elaborate effects, it will pay him to have a top row of lights above his proscenium, as well as his side illuminants. Tri-colour lighting, by which many wonderful effects can be obtained, is described more fully in *The Bankside Book of Puppets*, in the chapter on Lighting, but this can be done in a simple manner with the top row of light boxes. For this purpose there should be at least *five* boxes—the centre *red*, then on either side of this, one *green*, one *blue*, with the same again in reverse order, on the two outside lamps, *Figure* 27. These lamp boxes should be so arranged on their frame as to allow the easy changing of the colour screens in order that other tints, such as amber or purple, can be used if needed.

The *colour mediums* can be either *gelatine* or *celastoid*, the latter medium being less likely to crack up from the effects of heat. With both

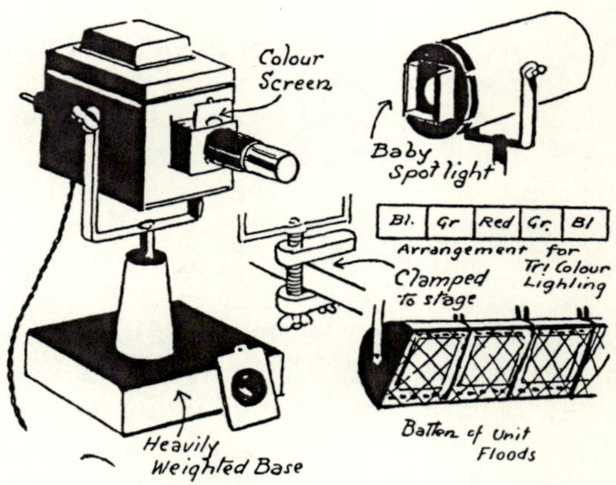

Fig. 27.—Spotlights, the tri-colour system, and flood batten.

of these mediums it is possible to obtain a very wide range of additional tints by superimposing one colour against another.

If the builder of the stage is not an experienced electrician, it is advisable that all the wiring and fitting up of the lighting system should be done by a practical man who thoroughly understands his trade. This is no job for an amateur, there is too much responsibility attached to the use of electricity for an important system like this to be put together by an unskilled hand and, as far as possible, the whole thing should comply with the rules and regulations for public safety already mentioned.

In *Figs.* 26 and 28 the wiring circuit of the London Marionette Theatre's travelling stage is shown in diagram form. Each light is on a separate lead and has its own plug. To each of the switches there is a plug, and one main switch controls the whole system. The outer switches on the top row are: 1—5, used for side lights, the three in the centre 2, 3, 4, for top lighting, and the isolated switch and point I for a mobile or pilot-light, which did duty for exterior lighting effect on interior scenes and for additional illumination on the back cloth, to disperse shadows thrown by properties or standing units.

No *dimmers* were used in this system because, as a rule, on a travelling show, which is nearly always a part variety performance, dimming effects are seldom required. If the producer requires a dimmer he can use either one of the regulation dimmers supplied by the firms who manufacture theatrical lighting apparatus, or he can use a home-made apparatus known as a *water dimmer*, or obtain his effect by an even more simple process, which consists of either a sheet of frosted glass in front of his gelatine colour medium, or the use of semi-frosted celastoid—which dispenses with the necessity for glass and *then*, to pass a thin metal or cardboard screen down behind the colour medium, or between the gelatine and the frosted glass. Both the water dimmer and

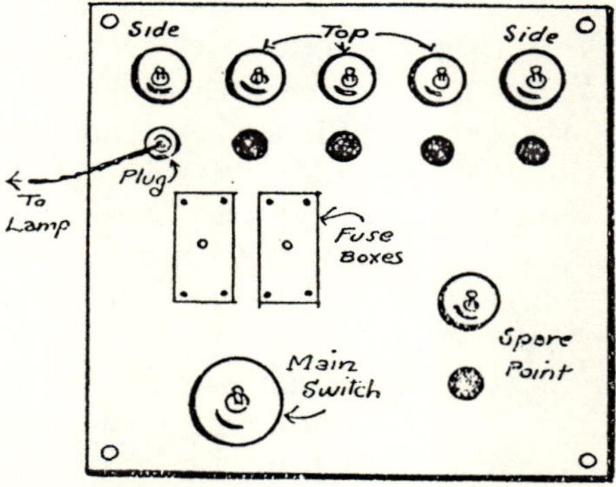

Fig. 28.—The switch board for a travelling fit-up.

screen method are illustrated in *Figure* 29. In the ordinary way, the screen dimmer is the most practicable for the travelling showman, because it takes up no room in packing and there is no chance of it being knocked over and its contents scattered about, or of being smashed in the course of transport.

All materials used should be of the best quality, and all parts where " live " wires occur must be protected. The switch board can be a separate unit from the cross bars that carry the system. Everything should be made to take apart as much as possible, and the switch board can be held in position by means of bolts and butterfly nuts, also the batten which carries the row of lamp boxes can be fitted up in the same manner.

It will be noticed, by a reference to the illustration of the batten, that each of the light boxes is fitted on to a pair of brackets which allow it to be tilted to any desired angle. Each box swings separately from its fellow, and this allows a very useful range of light beams on any particular part of the stage.

As the result of experiment, the producer will discover that many beautiful effects can be obtained by lighting on drapery and curtains. Certain materials will take on colour better than other kinds. Casement cloth will take on very good effects from colour lighting, and the producer will be surprised at the great range of colours that can be thrown on to ordinary black casement. Muslin is another material that has immense possibilities when lit from above or below, or at the sides. Coloured material, red or green, or other hues, can be intensified if a flood of the *same colour* is thrown upon them, and here, again, experiments with the tri-colour batten will bring some wonderful effects into being.

Clouds, white and coloured, can be thrown on to a sky by means of a piece of mottled or variegated glass held in front of a pilot-light and directed on to the back cloth.

Unless it is absolutely necessary to the

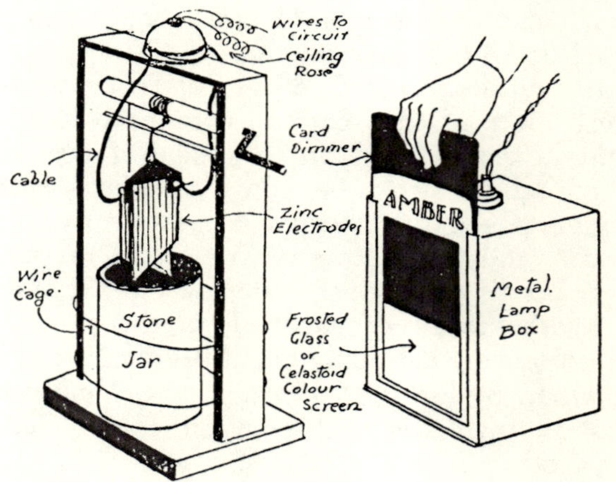

Fig. 29.—Water pot and cardboard dimmers.

action of a play, no exposed light should be visible to the audience, as this is extremely distracting. The same thing applies to the operators on the bridge to a certain extent, as an open light on the stage showing directly up into the eyes of the manipulator is likely to have a very detrimental effect on his control over the dolls. So that if all the lights are diffused through screens or frosted mediums, there will be little danger of suffering from eye-strain.

For lighting effects that are to be entirely separated from the main system, such as when a marionette enters carrying a lantern, or a candlestick with lighted candle is standing on a table, a camp fire, or a fire in a grate and so on, an ordinary 4.5 volts torch lamp and pocket battery will serve the purpose quite well. In the little play " Fly by Night," produced by the London Marionette Theatre, the watchman carries a lighted lantern, and the method by which the battery and lamp are fitted to the control and lantern is shown in *Figure* 30. Flex used for this sort of work should be as thin as possible, but at the same time very strong and not likely to snap, and cause a disconnection at a most inopportune moment. The writer has dismal memories of a trick fire, supposed to represent a bundle of twigs magically ignited by a fairy, and, in another scene a fire that is " put out " by the same personage. The same trick fire was used for both occasions and, to the tremendous disgust of the operators, when the fairy said: " Let us see what these twigs will do for us," the thing would light up and then go out immediately afterwards and remain out all the time it was supposed to be alight; or, when the fairy said: " There's no warmth in a fire like that—it's gone out," said fire simply refused to go out and remained alight in defiance. Only an experienced operator has any idea what it feels like to be on the bridge on such an occasion, and have to try and think out a gag of some

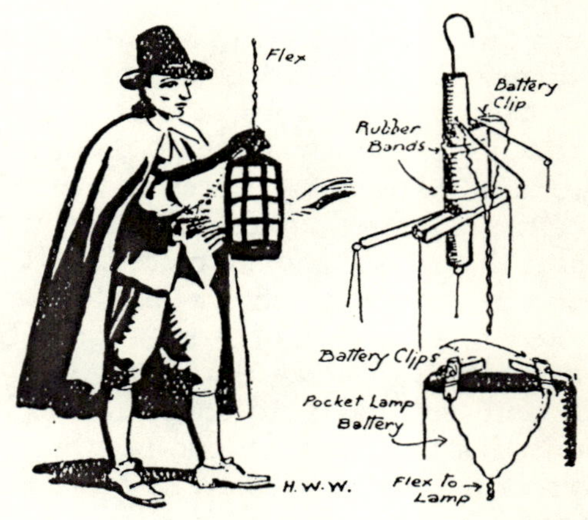

Fig. 30.—The night-watch, showing battery connections for the lantern.
A character by W. S. Lanchester.

sort to get one out of the difficulty. This thing happened again and again, became a regular occurrence, until, after a great deal of searching and rewiring, a tiny little break was discovered in the flex, and this was the cause of all the trouble ; after that a new piece of wiring was substituted. This was stiffer and, apparently, stronger, but the same trouble happened again after a day or so. Then it was discovered that this flex was *too stiff*, the wires broke off while the property was being placed on the stage. So a fresh lead of softer flex was fitted and all went well.

This " horrid example " will give some idea of the care which must be taken in the handling of all lighted properties. They should be tested before each performance, and the batteries too, for that matter, because they are likely to run out just at a time when they are wanted on the stage. So that it pays to keep always on hand a new spare battery, ready for an emergency, and a good plan is to buy the batteries in pairs, or to make a point of purchasing a new one as soon as the new stock battery is placed in action.

For the benefit of those readers who have little or no knowledge of electrical matters, this chapter will conclude with a very brief description of some of the electrical terms and tools likely to be met with. The author lays no claim to being a practical electrician, in the technical sense of the word, and there are plenty of books and works of reference dealing with this very complicated subject, that describe the matter far more fully than the limited space of this particular book will allow. Some of these books are mentioned in the bibliography at the end of this volume.

Electrical Terms

Conductor. The wire, copper or iron through which the electric current flows.

Insulator. A non-conductive substance through which the current cannot pass. Vulcanite, slate, china, rubber, ebonite and substances that contain compressed fibre, rubber or waxed paper. *Dry* wood is non-conductive, but if it is *wet* the current will pass through.

Ampere. The quantity of, or *rate of flow* of the current.

Voltage. The unit of pressure. The voltage marked on a lamp indicates that the current requires the pressure of that particular number of volts in order to get the maximum degree of efficiency from the lamp.

Watt. The unit of measure of the amount of *work* an electrical current will do.

Resistance. Certain wires offer resistance to electrical current according to their material. The current, when passing through some metals, becomes weaker in quantity than when it passes through a conductor metal, because these particular metals give a greater resistance to the current than the true conductors. The resistance of a conductor to a current is termed *Ohms.*

Currents are of two kinds, *Alternating* and

Direct. An Alternating current passes backwards and forwards, changing its direction with extreme rapidity, whilst a Direct current flows always in the same direction.

Workshop Flex. The best type of material to use for portable wiring.

Switches. Two types, "tumbler" and "knife." The knife switch should be avoided owing to the amount of "live" parts which are exposed.

It is possible to obtain fairly "silent" tumbler switches, this type should be used in order that unnecessary noises of back stage may be eliminated.

Fuses. Small pieces of thin wire inserted into insulated carriers and forming part of the circuit. At a certain temperature this wire melts, thus showing an excess of current and a possible danger of fire. The melted fuse breaks the circuit and prevents the possible danger.

Plugs. Connections between the fittings and the current. The socket into which the plug is fitted is known as a *point.*

Insulating Tape is used for covering joints and connections in cables and flex.

CHAPTER VI

MARIONETTES IN THE MAKING

The Head

IN a puppet, a well designed and accurately modelled head is an absolute necessity. It is the most noticeable part in the whole doll, just as a man's face and expression is that which attracts the primary attention of an onlooker.

If the marionette is "topped off," so to speak, with an inane, toy-doll like head and features, it will never look like anything else than a toy-doll, however well it may be dressed, or even acted. Whereas, if it be but a poorly costumed figure, with little or no movement at all, but yet with a finely modelled head, it will hold its audience and keep their attention, because it looks like an actual personage, a reality.

Some marionette makers, particularly those on the Continent, believe in making the head definitely on the large size. German and Czechoslovakian puppets are particularly noticeable in this respect. In some cases, perhaps, a big head may add to the appearance and character of a figure, but in the main the big head has one very great drawback in that it dwarfs the figure, giving it a kind of hydrocephaloid appearance in which all the growth has gone to the head, leaving the body and limbs to carry along as best they can.

On the Continent there are a number of firms who make marionettes of all descriptions

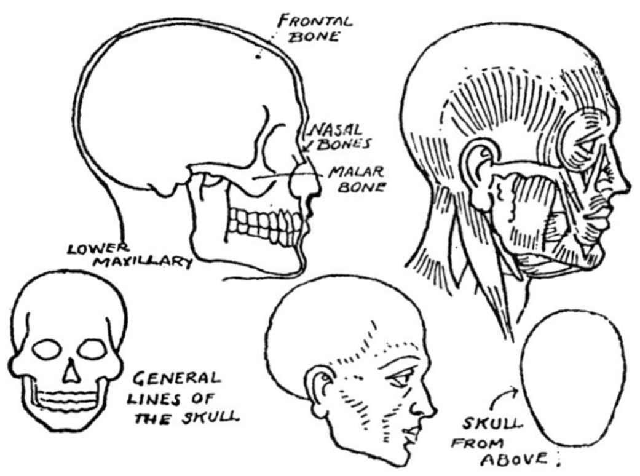

Fig. 31.—Anatomical details of the head.

for sale. In Italy there are several of these puppet manufacturers, and in Czechoslovakia there are notably, the firms of Modry and Zanda, and Kral, both of Prague. These people make their puppet heads in a form of plaster composition. They are finely modelled, with slightly exaggerated details and a very definite make-up. *Figure* 31 shows some heads of Continental dolls.

But, without a doubt, most people would prefer to model or carve their own heads, and it is by far the best way to do it, for however crude and inartistic their efforts may seem to be, there is this satisfaction, that one has done a thing for themselves. So, for the benefit of those who feel that they are handicapped by lack of knowledge, as well as artistic ability, the instructions that follow are especially designed.

The first, and most important matter to be mastered is *proportion*, and as far as the head and face are concerned, this is shown in the illustration (*Figure* 32). It will be seen that, on a side view, the head can be divided into *two* equal parts, the face and the cranium.

Notice, too, that the head very nearly fills the square, except just under the back of the skull. A front view of the head, however, can be divided into *three* equal parts and fits into a somewhat pear-shaped oval. Part *one* begins at the base of the hair line or top of the forehead and ends just below the eyebrows. Part *two* ends just beneath the nostrils, and part *three* terminates at the point of the chin.

The space between the two eyes is just about the width of *one* eye (*Figure* 33), and, as a rule, the corners of the mouth are immediately below the centre of the eyes.

To make a really careful study of the head

and face, and for the whole figure for that matter, a certain amount of anatomical knowledge is very necessary.

The superficial bones and chief muscles, which play such important parts in the contours of the figure, should be noted, sketched, and if desired, modelled by way of practice.

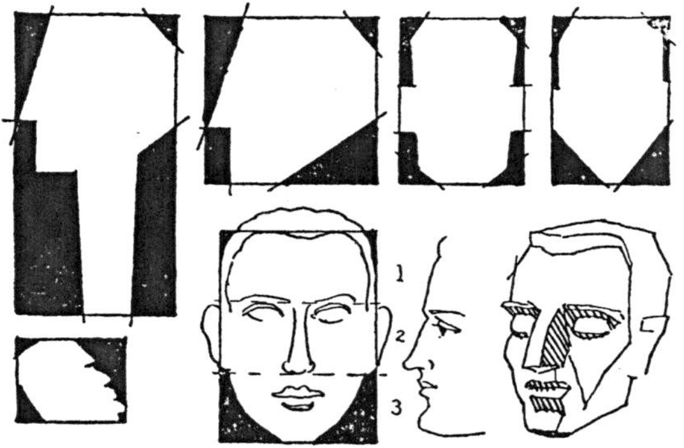

Fig. 32.—The head first cuts and proportions.

In the head, for example, the shape of the cranium, side view, front view, back view and especially from above, must be taken into consideration. The cranium from above is seen to be wider at the back than at the front and slightly flattened at the sides. There is a prominence on the forehead caused by the frontal bone, which, in some cases is developed to a very great extent, whilst in other cases it is quite a negligible thing. Notice the shape of the *back* of the skull and the small bumps behind the ears, caused by the mastoid processes of the olecranon; on the facial part of the head the zygoma, or cheekbone, the points of the upper and lower maxillaries. Jaw bones will have a tremendous influence upon the modelling of the head. Also the occiput bones above the eyes will affect the light and shade of the puppet's head to a very great degree. See *Figure* 31.

In *Figure* 31 the same views of the head are also shown, with the main muscles drawn in, and the effect of these main subcutaneous bones and the chief muscles upon the features is illustrated.

The best way for a beginner is to make studies and notes of the details here given, then to try and model, in a broad way, "sketch" heads in plasticine or modelling clay or wax. When it comes to the finished head, however, the best thing to use is a good piece of wood. American white-wood or lime, beech or birch are all good carving woods. Mahogany or walnut are not recommended because of their tendency to split. The block must be first cut into a rough shape with a saw, as shown, and the preliminary chisel cuts can then be made until the head assumes the general shape required, and all the main details, position of nose, eyes, etc., are in proportion. Then, if the head is to move on a separate neck, a hole about three-quarters of an inch to an inch in diameter will be drilled up into the head from the jaw—this hole must go well up into the head. After this the rest of the carving can be completed. If the head and neck are to be all one piece, then the preliminary cuts and shape will be as shown in *Figure* 32.

A very useful tool for this kind of work is a small tenon saw, and a " coping " saw will

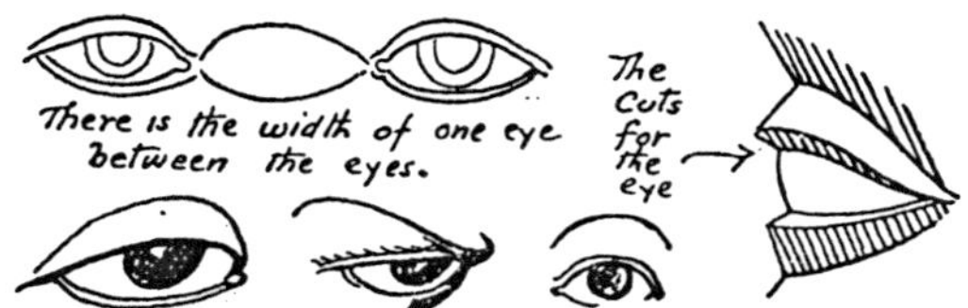

Fig. 33.—Proportion and details of eyes.

be found handy for a good many cuts that the tenon saw is unable to perform. If the worker has a decent bench-vice the business of carving and cutting will be made much easier, as the block can be held securely during the process, leaving both hands free.

Another useful tool is a rasp. One of the best types of rasp is that made by the firm of Tiranti, of Maple Street, London. The worker will begin to collect up various kinds of chisels and rasps and a particularly useful chisel is a one-eighth, as it can be used for cutting grooves and slots in parts where joints are to be made. At the end of this preliminary stage the head will appear as something like *Figure* 32, and from this point its final effect will be developed. If it is to be of a feminine type, the whole of the contours will have to be evenly modelled and the point of the chin made less rugged and more delicate, the cheek bones smoothed away and the occipetal protuberance less in evidence. If, on the contrary, the face is to be that of a hard featured, elderly man, all the smoothness of line will be gone, and heavy brows, prominent cheek bones, lines on either side of the mouth, and jaw and chin much developed. The worker always bearing in mind the fact that the figures are to be seen from a distance, will give prominence to this comparison between the sexes by the delicate lines of his female faces as contrasted with the hard lines and deep shadows of the males.

Before proceeding to the subject of Character and Facial Types, it will be as well to take the various parts of the head and face in detail and notice their particular points. The eyes, for instance; a bisecting line drawn across the eyes takes in each point. *Figure* 33 shows where the under lid goes *beneath* the upper lid. Such detail as this will hardly show on a small puppet's head, but the very knowledge of points of this description will largely influence the accuracy of effect in the carver's work. In the main, the eyes can be cut in as an impression rather than a detail, and *Figure* 33 is intended as a general guide in this respect.

Details of the nose are shown in *Figure* 34 and the drop back to the inner corner of the eye is especially important because, in a puppet's head this detail can be slightly exaggerated, in fact the whole eye can be well "sunk," the orbit fairly deep in order that a

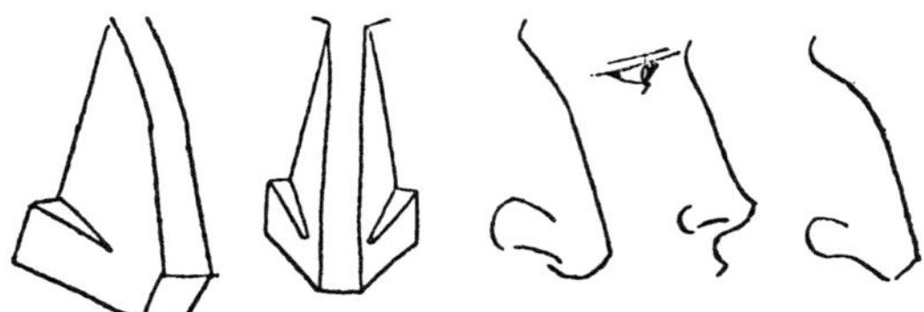

Fig. 34.—First cuts and details of the nose.

certain amount of shadow can be cast from the brows, thus giving a more realistic effect.

The nose should be well shaped, slightly prominent, but not too broad across. It plays a very important part in the casting of shadows on the face.

The minor details, nostrils, etc., can be carved or painted in when the face is finally "made-up."

The lips will be mainly of the "Cupid's bow" type, especially in the heads of female figures or children, and for clean-shaven men a very much modified form of the same pattern will look quite well.

The ears come roughly into the second of the three proportionate divisions of the face, the tops being about level with the brows and the lobes on a line with the base of the nose. In general form they consist of a large oval shape above, to which a smaller half oval is attached at the base. The inner moulding might be described as a curved Y shape, surrounding the aural orifice. In side view, the ear appears as in *Figure* 35.

In addition to noting and experimenting on the details laid down, the student should, if possible, make a point of studying pieces of antique and classical statuary, either in the actual form or by means of pictures and photographs. If it is possible to visit the Victoria and Albert Museum or any similar gallery, the carvings in marble, ivory, or in wood will be well worth a careful study.

To return to the rough blocked-out head (*Figure* 32), the sculptor had reached a point in which all the general proportions were set and the type of character decided upon, and apart from the main artistic end to be attained as a result of the carver's efforts, the rest of the work is entirely to do with the puppet's requirements, the technical details of the marionette's head.

The exaggeration of the eye sockets, either by protruding brows or sunken eyes, the prominent nose and under-lip-to-chin cut, the very definite cheek bones and other details can now be carved in, giving the head more definition and character.

The *neck* can now be made and fitted on. A pit or socket, for the neck piece has been drilled into the head block. This pit should be rounded off at the back of the head, and

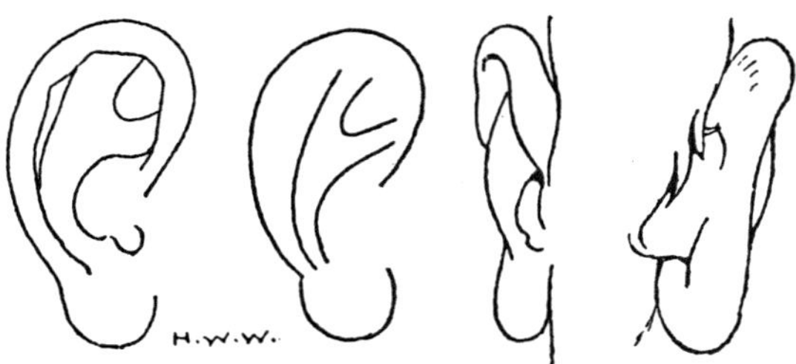

Fig. 35.—Details of the ear.

under the chin, until it becomes slightly egg-shape in appearance. This is to allow more freedom in the nodding movement so often required and to enable the head to look upward.

The neck should be shaped as shown in *Figure* 36, and has a small screw-eye in the top through which the wire bar will pass, that forms the connection between head and neck. If the neck itself is to be double-jointed, it will have either another screw-eye at its base or a hole drilled through for the bar that forms the body connection (*Figure* 36). In the case of bare-necked figures, it is best to carve the neck as a fixture, or part of the body, and to make the head move only, unless the joint can be made very carefully and neatly, in the manner as also shown in *Figure* 36.

Trick Heads, such as speaking heads, for example, are made on much the same lines as ventriloquial figures. Figures that can open and shut their mouths are very useful characters to have in a troupe. In most of the big professional troupes the speaking head is almost the general thing. The methods of producing this effect are shown herewith. The making of a head of this type requires a good deal of patience and skill.

A piece of wood is cut out of the face (with a fret-saw), taking away the bottom lip and the point of the jaw. A hole is drilled through the two sides of the jaw and in place of the piece cut away a lead jaw is substituted, which is pivoted on a pin put through the jaw and the lead. The worker must make sure that the pivot point of the lead jaw is so placed as to have the heavier part of the lead at the back to form a true counterbalance. The idea being that when the jaw string is pulled it *opens* the mouth, and as soon as the string is slackened the jaw shuts automatically by the downward movement of its heavier half.

The head is made in two pieces. A face piece with the jaw movements hollowed inside; and a back piece with hollow inside to let the counterbalance swing up and down. The string passes through a hole in the back piece, which also is made to screw on and off the front for purposes of regulating the strings or movements should any mishap occur. Some experts have a short length of *wire* running up from the counterbalance to a point just outside

Fig. 36.—Neck joints. (*a*) Traditional head and neck, one piece. (*b*) Fixed neck, head on a pivot. (*c*) Double action, neck and head pivoted.

the top of the head, where it terminates in a loop to which the string is attached. This wire saves the trouble of opening up the head should a string get broken, and means a quick repair in such an emergency. In operating a speaking doll a tremendous lot of practice is necessary, and very careful rehearsal of the words to be spoken, in order that the mouth opening actions of the puppet may coincide or synchronise with the voice of the speaker.

Apart from carved wood there are other ways of producing heads which may appeal to the craftsman.

The first method is that of papier mâché. This means a light-weight head, and as far as weight goes anything that will make for a general "lightness" of the figure is a good thing to take into consideration. In this method the head is first modelled in plasticine—the ordinary, non-setting type. All the details are very slightly exaggerated. Eyelids, nostrils, lips and so on, to allow for a true effect on the paper form when completed, as the modelling loses a little of its sharpness in the covering of paper layers.

After a satisfactory head is modelled, the worker proceeds to paste or glue small strips of very soft tissue paper—serviette paper is good for this sort of thing—*all over* the head as illustrated. When this has set, another layer is pasted on, *completely covering* the first layer. This process is repeated for about six layers and then the head is put by to dry. Incidentally, an excellent way in which to make sure that each succeeding layer covers its predecessor properly, is to use a *different coloured* paper for alternate pastings. After a few days, when the head is set and hard, it is sawn or cut into halves (*Figure* 38). The plasticine is removed and the halves joined together very carefully by glued strips of *linen* on the inside and repapering on the outside. The head can be glued to a round block of wood which goes right up inside to the top of the head, and can be either the neck of a fixed head, or it can be bored to make a hole for a movable neck joint (*Figure* 36).

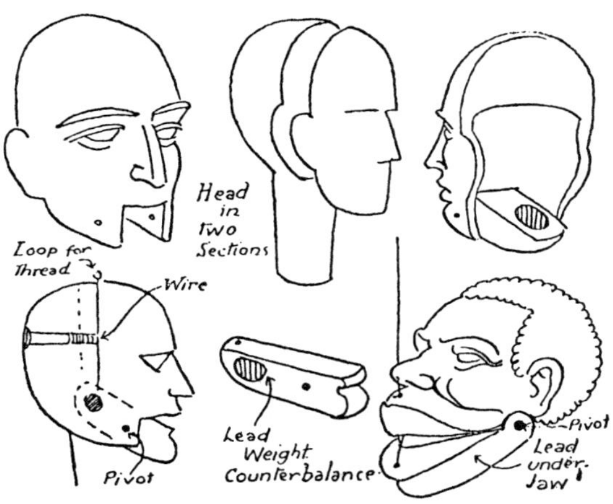

Fig. 37.—Speaking heads.

Another method is to make a rough block shape of the head in wood and then to model the features by hand in fausse barbotine, or some similar modelling clay which will set quite hard and not crack.

By a third method, the head is modelled first in modelling clay, wax moulds are then made from the pattern figure, and from these moulds impressions are taken in plastic wood. The important thing to remember, however, in taking these impressions, is that plastic wood shrinks slightly as it hardens, so that the first layer in the mould must be extremely thin and allowed to set before another layer is put on. The mask, or head, when completed is very thin but strong, and can be glued to a wood-block to finish the head. By this means *faces* can be produced and fitted to head blocks, and it follows naturally, that for repetition work—choruses, soldiers and supernumerary figures—a method like this is going to save a great deal of time.

CHAPTER VII

MARIONETTES IN THE MAKING—*contd.*

Make-up and Finish

THE puppet maker will have to decide whether he will sacrifice his model-making tendencies for the benefit of the back row of his "gallery," or let the gallery "go hang," and finish off his heads and details for the express benefit of the front row of stalls and such privileged persons who are allowed to go behind after a performance. All the time spent on making and painting carefully detailed and accurate modelled heads and hands is time more or less wasted, because to at least ninety per cent of the audience the delicacy of detail will be unrecognisable, "love's labour lost," so to speak.

Of course, if the puppets are being made for *film reproduction*, detail and finish *are* important, because the camera with its powerful lenses will take in all the small details, and these will be enlarged to a tremendous size when projected on to a screen, so that here, for instance, unfinished work and crudity of detail will be more than emphasised on the screen.

So that for the marionette maker the

important thing to be borne in mind will be to strike a happy medium, in which accuracy of detail and delicacy of line are entirely in agreement with a bold and broad treatment in the make-up. If possible, it would be greatly to the advantage of the craftsman to study the style and make-up of other producer's dolls, and take particular notice of the exaggerated expressions and definite colouring. The

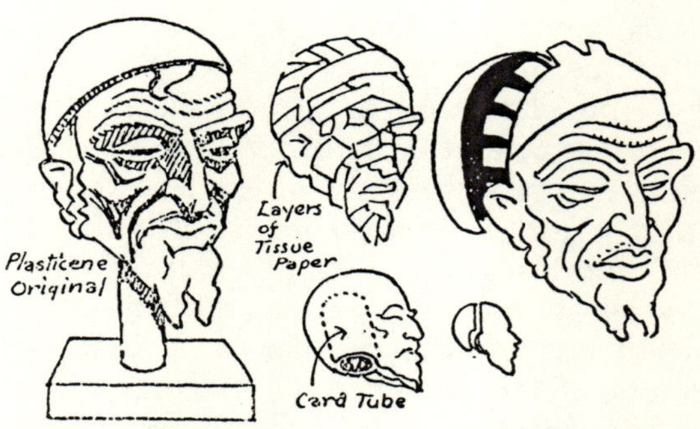

Fig. 38.—Method of making papier maché heads.

French Guignol Puppets, for example, with their broad patches of red on cheeks and lips and deep purple blue shading around the eyes. In a similar manner the Czechoslovakian marionettes are "made-up," eyes, lips and cheeks brought into prominence in a very definite manner, but not quite so broadly treated as the Guignol Puppets. These dolls can be seen by fairly large audiences and, as in both cases the operators are extremely skilful, the impression on the audience is very satisfactory. Contrasted with the broad manner of treatment is that adopted by other experts, such as the great Richard Teschner, whose puppets are small, extremely delicate in line and contour, and finished to the last degree in all the details of a jeweller's art. Miniature, and exquisite, wonderful works of a master craftsman—*but* to be seen by only a small audience, to the back rows even in ideal conditions the delicacy of detail is lost.

Painting. "Flat" oil colours make the best pigments for painting the hands, feet and faces of the puppets. Ordinary student's oil colours, sold in tubes by most art material dealers, with plenty of turpentine as a "thinner," and perhaps a little gold size will do the job effectively and well. *Light red* and *Naples yellow*, very, very little of the red is needed, make a good flesh tint for general use, and a touch of *vermilion* worked in on the cheeks and lips will add to the face the necessary detail.

The whites of the eyes should be a pale creamy, or greenish white, and the eyeballs a gradation in rings of either pale blue to dark purple, or light brown, golden brown, to black. There are experts who advocate the perfectly plain eye—no eyeball at all. They say that if the eye is made either concave or convex and well varnished the effect is more subtle and suggestive of movement than it is with the definitely painted eyeball. There is, certainly, much to say for the plain, *concave* eye, because there is a certain amount of shadow cast by the top half of the eye socket which, when the head is under strong lighting and in action, does really suggest a lot of movement. A pale *turquoise blue* is a very effective colour to use for these blank, socket-like eyes.

The colouring of the male faces should be

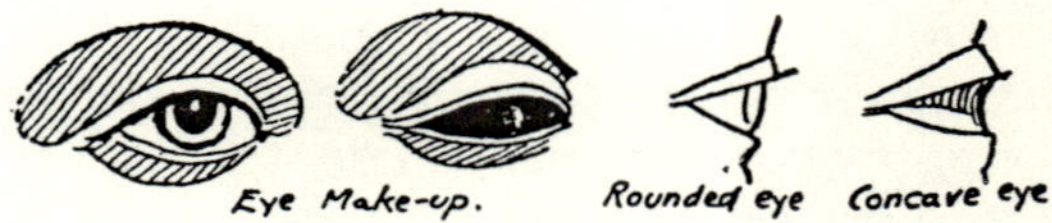

Fig. 39.—Make-up of eyes.

deeper and more robust than those of the females, which can be a pale creamy rose with very soft gradations of tint on the cheeks. This contrast of the sexes should be definite and pronounced, and if well done will add much to the general artistic effect. The Chinese puppet makers paint their female dolls' faces perfectly white and they look surprisingly delicate and feminine as a result. Practically all Oriental puppets have these distinctive face colourings, some even being painted green and yellow to give definition to the character they represent. Goblins, sprites, or fantastic creatures of any description can be painted almost any colour that the producer likes, but it is well to bear in mind that a great deal of character and atmosphere can be *appreciated by the audience* if the dolls have about them that *sense* in their colouring that conveys across the footlights just the type of personality they are supposed to represent. *Green* is cold and jealous. *Purple* is mystic and strange. *Red* and *orange* are warm and strong and vigorous, and suggestive of health and vitality. *White*, again, is suggestive of purity and nobility; while *black* is a type of the exact opposite. Not that one would suggest that all the villains should have black *faces* any more than all the mystics should have purple ones. The latter suggestion is done more with the aid of lighting than face colouring. But, where possible, the *idea* can be introduced by means of black hair against a white face, and all-black clothes and so on.

This hint of colours and their meanings is introduced at this point in order to set the puppeteer to thinking about these things, and making it his or her business to hunt up a little more about the subject in the local library. The use and arrangement of colours will play such a tremendous part in almost everything the artist will be doing for the theatre, that a working knowledge of the science is an absolute necessity, and the possession of it or any part of it, a definite step on the road to future success.

"Make-up" of a simple kind is certainly necessary. Not that the dolls will need to be made-up for every show like actors on the human stage, but just as an actor darkens round the eyes and accentuates the lips and so forth, the eye surrounds of the puppets will bear a faint blue grey or a purplish tint, not too definite or it will look overdone. *Very little* ultramarine and light red with a good deal of Naples yellow will do the trick, and a darker line on the underneath part of the top eyelid will help to keep the eyeball from "staring." Pop-eyed puppets are all right for their special parts, but you don't want the whole troupe to look like it, therefore a quietness about the eyes, a restful look on some of the faces is a thing to aim at and attain, so that if one's puppets are really things of beauty they will most assuredly be a joy for ever.

Eyebrows should be dark *always*, even on a very fair doll, because fair eyebrows will hardly show under stage lighting unless they be gilded, then, perhaps, they will flash as the light strikes them. A good sable "liner" or signwriter's brush, very small in size, will be a fine pencil for putting on the eyebrows and give a very beautifully curved line if handled well.

Vermilion has been mentioned already as a lip colouring, and when painting the female lips in particular, the "Cupid's bow" effect should be very clearly defined (*Figure* 40). On children's heads the same effect must be attained. The male lips are "harder" in character.

"Blue" chins and "drawn" sickly faces will be obtained by a careful grading use of the blue-grey eye make-up already mentioned.

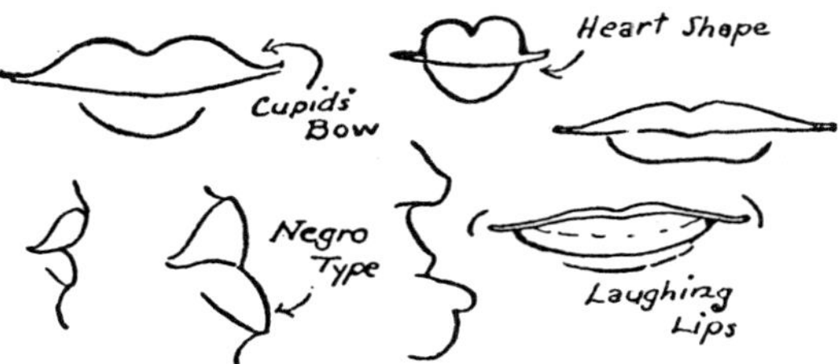

Fig. 40.—The lips.

Of course, a great deal of the actual character and expression of the head has been, or should have been, carved or moulded on the head itself so that the make-up artist will have no very difficult task to do in his painting, *but* the important thing to remember and never forget is that the front row of the audience will be at least eight feet away from the dolls and the back row twenty, thirty, forty or perhaps fifty feet beyond it.

A very good plan is to do *all* the make-up, painting, and scenery as well, under artificial light, for what looks bright, clean and colourful under such conditions will look as well if not better under stage lighting, and very often things that are painted in most brilliant colours in the daylight are a failure as regards brilliancy under artificial illumination.

Hair. Choice of material for puppet's hair must be left to individual taste. There are several ways of suggesting hair. Crepe hair, as used on the actual stage, is favoured by some puppeteers, and hair of this type or wigs of real hair was extensively used in the olden days. But all this kind of material though extremely effective, is likely to suffer from the ravages of time. It gets very drab and frowsy in appearance, and if it happens to be made of stranded wool it becomes a happy hunting ground for moths should the doll be put away for a time. The best type of hair is either carved directly on to the wooden head or modelled by hand in plastic wood or some similar material. An important point to remember, however, is that all modelled hair must be affixed to a roughened surface in order to " key " it to the wood. The big advantage of " effect " hair is that it can be painted and washed and kept in condition much easier than it is possible to do to the " real " type of hair.

CHAPTER VIII

MARIONETTES IN THE MAKING—*contd.*

Bodies

THERE was a time when puppet makers made their marionette bodies out of linen or wash-leather and stuffed them with sawdust or bran, but in more than one case of this description if moth and rust did not spoil the looks of the costumes, the rats and mice certainly made a fine mess of the figures, and it takes but one experience of this kind of tragedy to knock all future ideas of stuffed bodied marionettes out of a craftsman's head. In fact, the stronger and more permanent a puppet's body can be the better, and if it *can* be a nicely shaped and proportionate affair at the same time, all the more credit to its maker.

The most effective type of body is that with a waist joint. It is immaterial what method is employed to make the connection, though it follows naturally that it must be well and truly done. Of the types illustrated in *Figure* 42, the author prefers that with the double loops of cord, particularly for puppets used in play production because there are no metal parts to click and make unnecessary noises, and also because when the figure is seated there is just that sinking or slackness given to the figure which occurs when a real person sits in an easy chair and automatically relaxes.

The twin screw-eye joint was a favourite method of old-time craftsmen. It is very reliable if the screw-eyes used are substantial

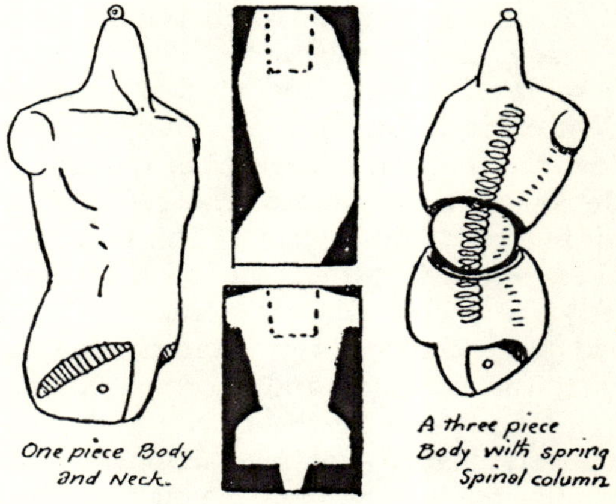

Fig. 41.—Body types and first cuts.

enough, but it has the disadvantage already mentioned of making sounds when the doll is in action.

For a doll that takes only a minor part in a play, and from which no great demand in the way of action is to be made, the body can be a single block of wood—a one-piece body. In a specified example in which the author and his partner were producing a shop scene, the doll for the shopman being behind a counter during the whole time of his appearance on the stage had, not only a solid wooden body, but also straight, unjointed legs with fixed feet. The whole scope of the doll's actions was confined to the head, arms and hands—

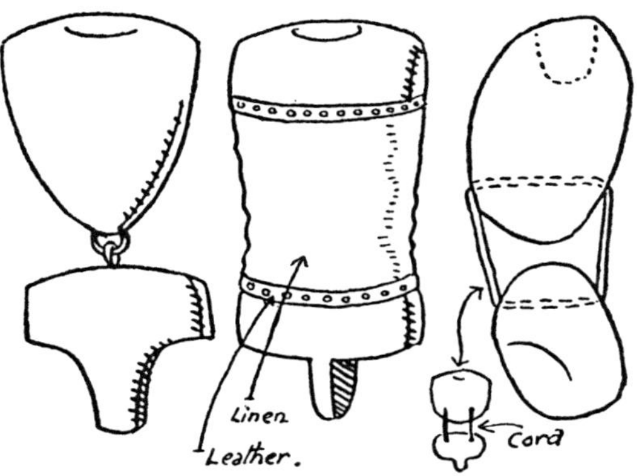

Fig. 42.—Types of waist joints.

the top half of the figure—and the result was a complete success.

This specialising of movement must be borne in mind at all times. A true marionette should be designed to do *one* or more very *definite things*, and to do them properly—*not* to do *anything* and *everything*. A marionette that can walk a few steps and then sit down on a chair in a natural, easy manner is a success, even if it is incapable of doing anything else; it is every bit as good a doll as one that can dance, and wave its arms about and stand on its head, and a dozen other things.

The wonderful dolls of Professor Skupa,

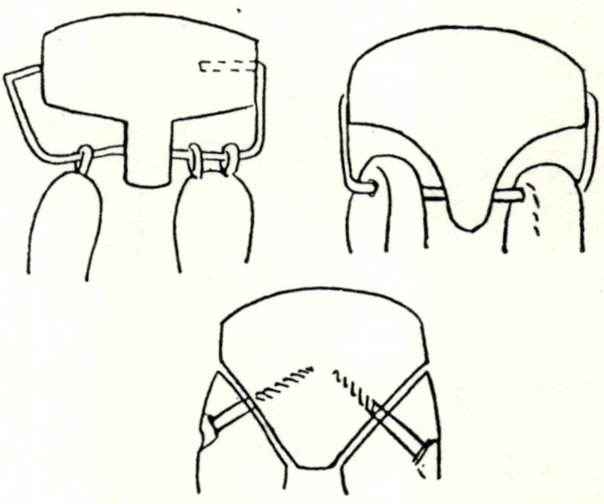

Fig. 43.—Thigh and hip connections.

mentioned in Chapter II, the Czechoslovakian puppet master of the Arts Theatre, Pilsen, appear to *think* before they act, their movements are so deliberate and definite, yet, in appearance, they are but caricatures of human beings. The whole secret of this being in the specialised movements for which the puppets are made.

So the importance of design and specialisation cannot be over-rated and, of a certainty, it must never be lost sight of.

Now, in the construction of the bodies *white wood* or *deal* will do perfectly well for the upper and lower sections, and if a screw-eye connection is to be made at the waist it will be well to put a little "seccotine" or glue of this description on each screw before fixing it into the wood.

The cord jointed bodies will need a strip of strong linen, soft and not too stiff, put round the space where the cord occurs, and so connecting up the two sections to form a completed body.

The first thing to do after the top section has been roughly shaped will be to make a pit or socket in which the lower end of the neck can articulate. This can be done by means of a brace and a three-quarters or one inch bit, as illustrated in *Figure* 41, which shows also the preliminary cuts and shape of the body. If the craftsman is unable to get wood of sufficient thickness, he can build up his body in sections, glued and nailed together. If he chooses he can leave the front part of the neck socket open, a detail which allows considerable scope for a forward movement of the neck, very useful in grotesque or comic characters where a sudden lurching forward of the head and neck is an asset. This front opening is covered eventually by the costume of the puppet, which being comparatively loose allows this neck movement to take place quite freely. The lower end of the neck should be rounded off to a blunt point, and may have either a hole drilled through near the base, for the connecting pin to pass through, on which the

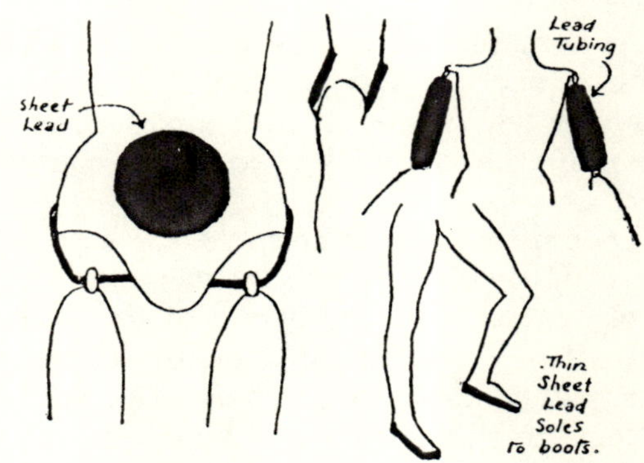

Fig. 44.—The positions of the weights to maintain the balance of the doll.

neck will move, or it can be finished with a screw-eye, strongly fixed, which answers the same purpose (*Figure* 36).

For silent movements the hole *through* the neck is to be preferred, and also the use of a strong wooden "skewer" rod as a pivot.

The method of connecting the neck to the body is demonstrated in *Figure* 36.

Coming to the under half of the body, the thigh and leg connections. The craftsman will meet again with more than one method of doing the job. The simplest form, however, is that of having screw-eyes in the ends of the top leg sections, and fixing them by passing a stout wire through the screw-eyes as well as through a hole drilled in the forepart of the pelvis, then bending the two ends *up* at right angles and turning them in to the top of the thigh (*Figure* 43). This method allows of a tremendous lot of movement in the legs and is particularly useful for very active puppets.

Walking dolls can have their legs connected by a pin passing through a hole in the top leg or two screw-eyes side by side (*Figure* 43), using a skewer rod for a pivot as in the neck. The single screw-eye joint or wire pivot allows too much side movement to get a good effect of walking. The legs should be made to move directly forward and not to turn sideways. This is another case in which the craftsman will probably find ideas of his own coming into action; experiments and tests will alone guide him as to the particular method to use for each different doll.

For a third type of joint, and one which seems a pretty simple matter, the connection between body and legs is made by cutting a slit in both body and top legs and a piece of strong leather used as the "link."

Again, there is the way of cutting the base of the body off at an angle (*Figure* 43) and making the top legs section to correspond with this angle, joining the two together by means of a strong screw driven in as shown.

But whatever the method used to connect the lower limbs to the body, great care must be taken to see that both legs are the same

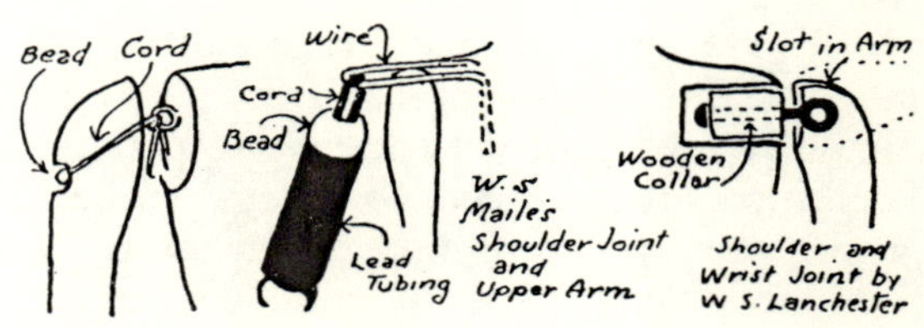

Fig. 45.—Shoulder joints.

length when finally fixed, that both feet rest flat on the floor when the figure is held up and that the thigh joints when completed are strong and permanent.

A point of *balance* now occurs. It is a very easy thing for the action of the legs to cause the lower half of the body to swing forward instead of remaining in position. To counteract this swinging, two small discs of sheet lead about the size of pennies are cut and nailed one on either side of the lower body section, as shown in *Figure* 44. This acts as a drag and counter-pull to the forward leg movement and gives also an excellent balance and poise to the body.

CHAPTER IX

MARIONETTES IN THE MAKING—*contd.*

Arms and Legs

THE secret of a successful arm is *flexibility*. Incidentally, this same remark applies to *all* joints of the figure. Stiffness means tragedy to a marionette, it means uncertainty to the operator, who never knows whether his doll will do the right thing at the right moment, or whether a joint will refuse to work at all at the time when its action is most required, but this freedom of movement is needed in the workings of the arm more than in any other part of the puppet with the exception of the head.

To the arm there are *three* definite joints, the *shoulder*, the *elbow* and the *wrist*. The wrist connection is dealt with in the instructions given on the *hand*.

The shoulder is the pivotal point of the whole arm and the joint should be so constructed as to allow the arm to move in any and every direction, up, down, out straight, across the front of the figure and round to the back if necessary. This means an especially flexible connection and one which will give absolute confidence to the operator.

To a certain extent the shoulders present a problem, that is, to get all this facility of movement and at the same time to give the true *shoulder effect* to the doll. The author's

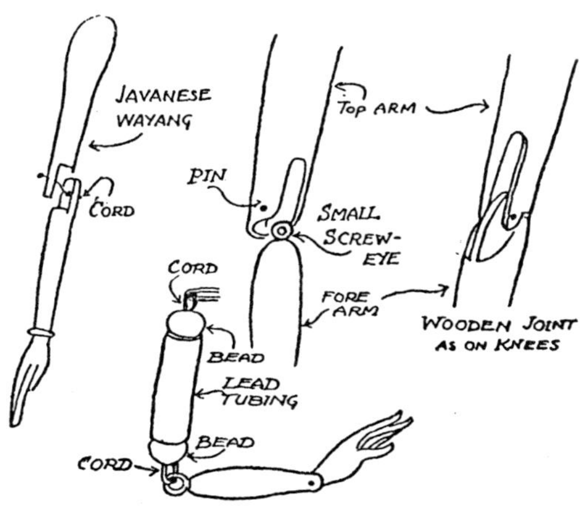

Fig. 46.—Elbow joints.

partner in the London Marionette Theatre, Mr. W. S. Lanchester, is a man of exceptional ingenuity, and he has devised a "collar" joint which has proved very successful, especially on dolls with bare arms. This connection is illustrated in *Figure* 45. It has the advantage that the arm can be taken right out and replaced if necessary, and for this reason the same joint is used on the wrist in some figures to permit the easier dressing of the figure.

Other experts favour a twin screw-eye joint with the screw-eyes interlocked or joined together with strong cord (*Figure* 45). Again, others prefer a single screw-eye put in to the body and a hole drilled through the top arm at the shoulder through which a cord with a bead on the end is passed and which is tied to the screw-eye, but not too tightly, so as to allow plenty of "play." A variation of this method is developed by Mr. W. Stanley Maile, in which the wire loop is bent in horseshoe fashion and again at a right angle, then the ends are driven into the body on the *top* of the shoulder (*Figure* 45). To this loop are fixed the cords of the top arm joint, which in this particular case consists of a lead-tubing bead held into position by two wooden beads through which the cord or bootlace is passed. This is shown in detail in *Figure* 46, and is a joint much preferred by puppet makers on account of its flexibility. The heavy top arm makes a splendid counterbalance to the forearm when in action, and allows the hand to be brought up to the face or against the body without any hitch, which an all wooden arm is often incapable of doing.

Other arm joints, especially at the elbow are illustrated in *Figure* 46. There is the all-wooden arm which will need either a locking joint exactly like that used for the knee, or a diagonally cut joint. There is also the type used by the puppet makers of Java. It will be good practice for the craftsman to test these different connections, because a joint which is suitable in some cases may be perfectly useless in others.

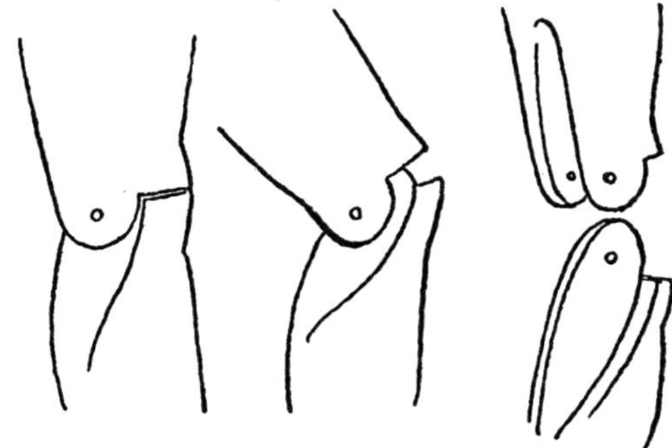

Fig. 47.—Knee joints—the locking joint.

For *knee* joints one type, and one only, is recommended, that is the locking joint already mentioned (*Figure* 47). The diagram shows the various stages of cutting and making this connection, and as a considerable amount of hard work is expected of this joint, it follows, naturally, that a good bit of wood, American white wood, for example, should be used for both top and bottom sections. When this joint is made it should be tested thoroughly in its movements, for perfect freedom of action is of the greatest importance here.

The methods of connecting the legs with the thighs are open to a good deal of variation. The joint can be made with wire and screw-eyes, see Chapter VIII, *Figure* 43, or a hole bored through the top leg section for the wire to pass through, but this latter method is useless for clowns or acrobatic figures.

Some craftsmen like *two* screw-eyes at the top of the leg joint for walking figures, others favour a piece of strong leather fixed into grooves cut into both thigh and leg. Leather has, of course, this disadvantage, that in time it may perish and rot, and that suggests the possibility of a leg falling off at some inopportune moment.

However, the craftsman can choose his own particular fancy out of the styles given, or perhaps he will invent an entirely new method or a more advanced development of an existing type. The chief thing to be certain of is that the joint works easily with absolute freedom from hold-ups and is *absolutely silent*, no squeaks or clicks to irritate the susceptibilities of a keyed-up audience.

Hands and Feet

For puppetry purposes hands can be

classified into two distinctive types—*speaking hands* and *holding* or *gripping hands*. In the first class are the simple, open palms, and others in which the index finger is used to suggest attention.

In the second class are hands which are definitely carved as if grasping an object and which are used when puppets are required to hold such things as swords, staves or household

Fig. 48.—Ankle joints.

articles. A glance at these types as illustrated will explain all this in a much more simple manner than all the words in the world.

Hands, and feet too for that matter, are best carved out of fairly hard wood and, if they are to be of the gripping class the matter of " grain " will have to be taken into consideration, because nobody wants to spend a lot of time on carving a hand, only to find it split when the finishing cuts are being put in.

Beech or birch are both good woods for the job. Mahogany is easy to cut, but has a tendency to split. Deal is too soft, unless the hands are very simple in shape and fairly large in size.

Before any attempt at carving is made, however, it will be well for the worker to get a general idea of the structure and formation of the hand. With a good working knowledge ready to hand, the whole business is going to be made considerably easier and the ultimate results far more satisfactory.

Looking at the hand from an anatomical and proportional point of view, the chief points to notice will be the positions of the joints in relation to one another, the length of the fingers in comparison to that of the thumb and to the back of the hand (*Figure* 46), the breadth of the hand in comparison to its length and the curves suggested by the positions of the joints.

A good deal of very valuable information is suggested in the diagrams, and if the craftsman can get *some* of this knowledge at his fingers' ends, he will find this business of hand carving a much more easy job than it appears to be.

When carving it will be best to *block out* the shape, quite roughly at first, making sure of the general proportions of fingers to back and of total length to breadth. A lot of carvers suffer from a sort of " podgy " complex when it comes to carving hands and feet, but particularly hands, they make them far too thick through and with fat fingers. It will add much to the grace and beauty of the hands if they can be slightly on the long-fingered side and thin and fairy-like, particularly the hands of the women and children.

A very handy and necessary tool for this

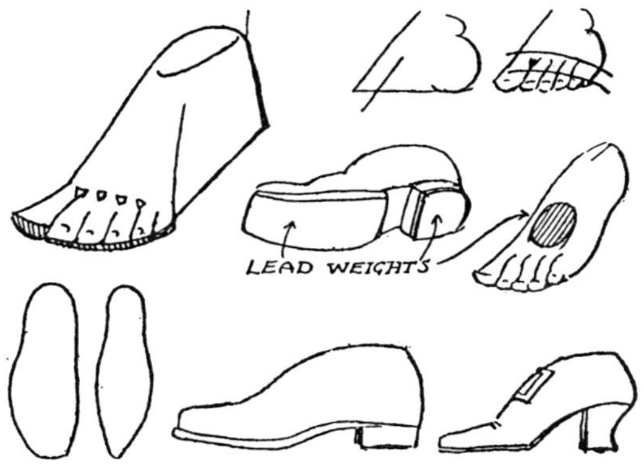

Fig. 49.—Feet in detail.

job is a small bench vice, a good fret-worker's vice will do in an emergency, but something a shade stronger, clamped or bolted down to the bench, will be a third hand holding the little block whilst the carver has both hands free and, in consequence, has a better control over the cuts he makes. A wood file, especially a

Tiranti "medium" rasp, is a splendid asset for roughly smoothing off and rounding edges, also a very small carving chisel, and V-shaped gouge, as well as a good chipping knife, are very useful for the fingers. Some experts separate the fingers by making saw cuts between them, but there is one very big point of danger about these separated fingers, and that is they give the hand a tendency to catch into the leg strings when the doll is in action, and some awkward moments are likely to occur when things like that happen during a show. The best types of hands are shown in *Figure* 50, in which the fingers are merely suggested by deep grooves cut into the hands.

Then there is the all-important *wrist joint*, a tremendous amount of effect and great possibilities of beauty in movement are dependent upon a good action here. With the hands the puppets *speak*, here is indeed a case in which "actions speak louder than words."

There are a number of kinds of wrist connections, most of them are illustrated in *Figure* 50, but *in every case* one important detail must be made perfect and that is complete freedom of movement. The action must be so easy that if the arm is held in the fingers and moved or tilted in various directions, the hand will drop without the slightest hesitation.

Great care will have to be taken that when

this joint is painted the pigment is not put on too thickly to clog and interfere with the movements and, when dressing the figure, this same care must be used to see that the cuffs of sleeves, for example, leave the action free. The wrist joint is one of the vital points of a marionette, and the best types of wood should be selected, especially a hard, non-splitting

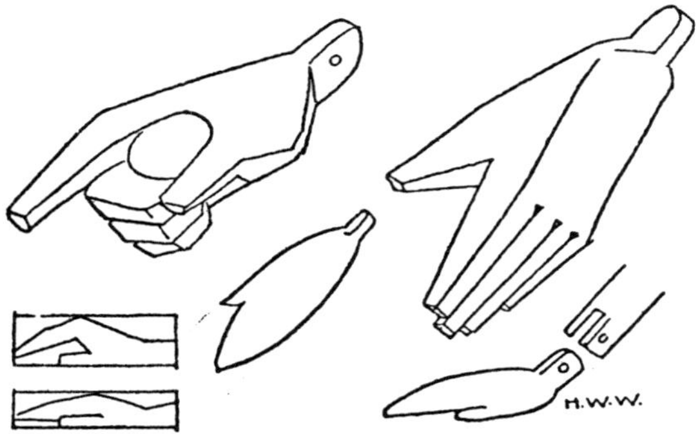

Fig. 50.—First cuts in hands, etc.

variety with a horizontal grain, if any, for the lower arm, in which the socket for the hand joint fits. A fine fret-worker's drill will be the tool for the worker to make the holes for the wire pivots, and both "mortice" and "tenon" should be smoothed with fine sand-paper before the actual joining takes place.

Feet. A well-shaped foot is as necessary and important to a puppet as a graceful hand.

A marionette that not only stands securely, but has a neat and shapely appearance about the feet and ankles, is going to give a great deal more pleasure to the audience and less trouble to the operator than a doll with ugly feet and an uncertain base on which it rests.

It follows then that a certain amount of anatomical knowledge will be in this case, as well as the hands, a real asset to the carver, even though ninety per cent of his feet will be cut with their boots already on. The necessary information is given, therefore, in simplified form in *Figure* 49, and the same information is put to practical use in the diagram illustrating the preliminary cuts to be made when carving the feet. If the feet are to be bare, take particular notice of the curves of the toe joints and of the slight hollow on the inner side of the foot. These details are important in giving a right and left appearance to the feet. Keep the *toes well pointed*, especially in the female feet, aim always at a graceful line, a " streamline " as the car manufacturers say.

The instep should be carefully studied and kept a little higher on the female feet than on those of the men. But in *every case* flat-topped feet should be avoided.

The Ankle Joint. There are two ways of making an ankle joint. The one with a slot in the foot or socket, and the corresponding tab on the leg as in *Figure* 48. The other way being the exact opposite, with the tab on the foot and the slot in the leg. Both ways are good and it is a matter of choice which method one uses. For bare feet the latter type is excellent as the outer sides of the joint can be used to suggest the ankle; but for booted feet

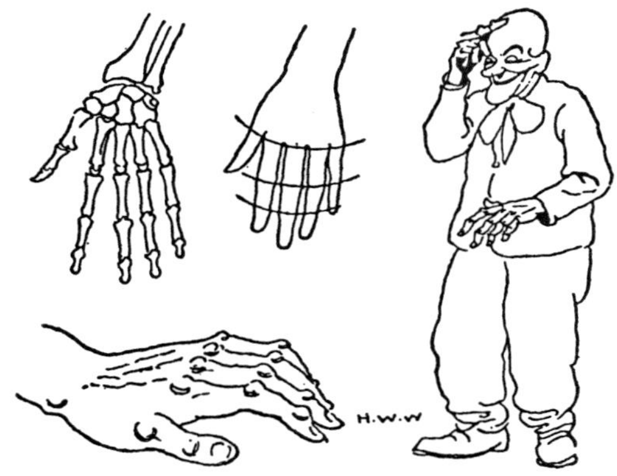

Fig. 51.—Hand anatomy, and the old man with articulated hands, a masterpiece by W. Stanley Maile.

the first mentioned method is very good, and if the figure is arrayed in Hessians, or high boots of any kind, the folds and creases about the ankle can be carved on the leg to correspond with the foot.

But whatever type of ankle joint is used, it is important that the joint must not be too loose and allow the feet to hang down or swing about too much, as it makes for a nasty effect of the feet dragging along the floor as if the puppets had a broken ankle, to say nothing of the extra effort needed to lift the leg higher in order to counteract this dragging.

If the figure is on the light-weight side the wooden feet can have a thin strip of *sheet lead* nailed or screwed to the soles to act as a counter-pull and balance (*Figure* 49). (For very small puppets up to ten or twelve inches in height lead feet entirely are recommended.) Booted feet should have very definite heels and, if possible, welts to the soles. In some cases the lead sheeting can be used as a distinct sole and be just a shade wider than the foot to suggest the welt.

For a marionette whose movements are to be particularly silent, felt shoes, with wash-leather or thick felt soles, are recommended, and when making these, as in all other parts of the puppet where cloth or leather or felt is used, it will be well to cut out a paper pattern, a template of the detail first for a try-out, otherwise a lot of costly material can be cut to waste.

CHAPTER X

Controls and Strings

WITH the marionette completed and all its parts joined together, the thoughts of the craftsman will turn immediately to the all-important subject of " Strings."

The threads themselves, or " wires " as some writers are pleased to call them, can be dealt with in a very few words. They must be *thin*, but they must be *strong*, as in the majority of cases they will have to stand a great strain, as well as a tremendous amount of wear and tear, especially the " run through " and leg strings.

A good, strong *carpet thread* (No. 18 for preference) may be used on puppets up to about two feet in height and a fine twine or stronger quality thread for dolls above this height. When the puppet is fully strung these strings should be rubbed well with a lump of beeswax, a process which will add considerably to their length of life and also prevent them from getting " frayed " and ragged. This waxing should be done to all strings at intervals.

But, before any single string can be fixed to a figure, a *control* or perch will have to be made. From this control the puppet will hang, and by its aid the majority of the marionette's movements will be produced.

Now there is a very fine array of these controls from which the puppeteer can make a choice, and the chances are a million to one that whichever type is adopted, the operator will speedily introduce his own ideas on the matter, and invent some gadget or " improvement "

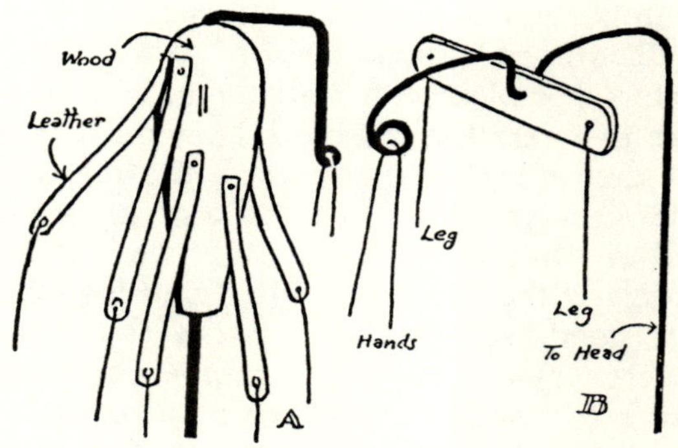

Fig. 52.—Main head-wire controls.
(*a*) Italian. (*b*) Czechoslovakian.

to the thing, which in *his* personal and private opinion is the last word in ingenuity, and a hundred per cent brainy bit of work.

In principle, however, apart from the brain-waves, these controls can be divided into several distinct types which will be described in detail, beginning with the early and simplest forms in order to avoid mental confusion when the stringing gets more complicated.

To dangle an object on the end of a bit of string must be as simple a way of controlling its movements as is possible, and that is exactly how a good many people control their dolls. In many Continental theatres the string is replaced by a more or less stout wire, according to the size of the puppet. This string or wire is fixed to the top of the head, and the end of it is held by the operator. In this manner the famous marionettes of Liege in Belgium are operated, and a wonderful amount of realistic movement can be obtained by the manipulators in these theatres.

Incidentally, some of these dolls are nearly three feet in height and of solid, carved wood, including the armour. At the International Exhibition of Marionettes at Liege in 1931, however, there was one of these three-feet, wooden, single wire dolls, made by Mr. Closon, which was dressed from head to foot in a wonderful suit of brass armour.

In this form of control the arms hang loosely, but with the marionette in the hands of an expert these arms are capable of a great deal of very expressive movement. At the top end the wire is bent into a sort of right angled hook by which the doll is hung on to the bridge when on the stage, but out of action, and also when off the stage.

From this very primitive control the addition of strings to the hands means but a single step, and so another type of control has the wire still, but it is bent over at the top in the form

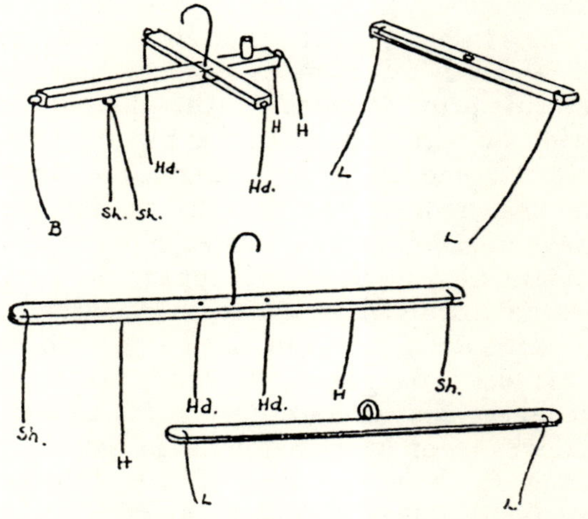

Fig. 53.—Old type English horizontal controls.

of a loop through which a run-through hand string can pass. A run-through string is one which passes from one hand or knee or shoulder, *through* a screw-eye or loop, down to the opposite hand, etc., on the other side of the figure. This widens the scope of the puppet's activities, which become wider still when two knee strings are added. Czechoslovakian puppets are operated in this manner. But here the wooden crossbar makes its appearance, for these knee strings are fixed to a small crossbar and this being moved up and down, or "rocked" by the fingers, causes the walking movement to occur in the puppet.

In some of the old Continental pictures a control wire with a head, and loops for the extremity strings, is shown as in *Figure* 52. But this is an obsolete form of manipulation and hardly worth the modern artist's time and trouble.

We come now to the all string types of control. The wire to head or back is superseded by strings and entirely disappears. First, then, the "Old English" control. This consists of two *separate* horizontal bars, on one bar the knee or foot strings, on the other bar the whole of the rest of the strings, head, shoulders, back and hands. Occasionally a short rod stuck out of the middle of this main bar to take the back string, but many of the perches did not have this fitting at all. Nearly all of them had a bent-wire hook arrangement on the main bar on which the leg bar which had a wire loop was hung.

Next comes the horizontal crossbar control shown in *Figure* 53. It is a very simple affair and, for marionettes up to about ten or twelve inches in height is a very good type to use. It will be seen from the illustration that it is really a development of the "Old English" control, with a back string bar to which a projection in front is added to bring the hand strings forward, and to separate them from the main group of strings. A further

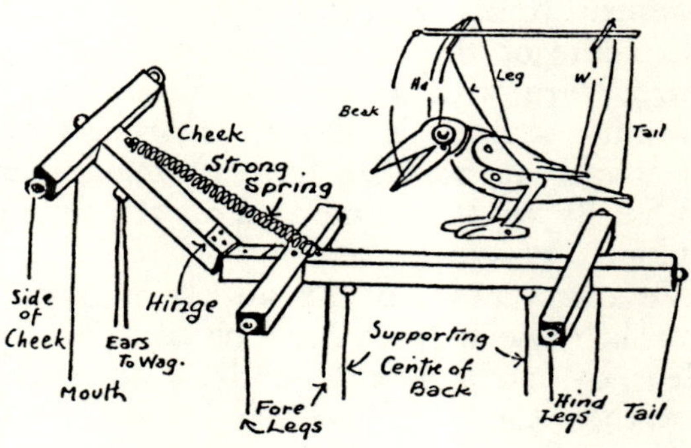

Fig. 54.—Animal controls.
Horse (L.M.T.). Bird (French).

development of this perch has a removable leg bar. All perches have a wire supporting hook used for hanging up the doll when not in use.

Another very different type of control is used largely on the Continent for fully stringed marionettes. Its principles will be better understood by reference to the diagram (*Figure 55*) than through the medium of a long description. It is an *upright* control, and for the purposes of this book will be known as the "Continental" control. The puppet is supported by two main strings to the top of the back, a little way below the shoulders and the two strings to the head. The shoulder strings join the control at the end of a sloping peg or bar, about three inches in length, which is fixed to the main rod or hand grip about three inches up from the bottom, and just below the point where the crossbar for the head strings is fixed (*Figure 55*) at *right angles* to the shoulder bar. The head bar is short, three or four inches in length, and *must be fixed securely* to the hand grip. A good plan is to cut a slot in the hand grip and set the bar in it, a sort of mortice and tenon joint.

Then, *above* the space allowed for the hand, there is another bar which should be made to either rock up and down or take off completely. This is the leg bar and if it is to be taken off for dancing purposes, should be about twelve inches long, or if a fixture for rocking, can be about half that length and used for walking only. An important point as regards the strings themselves occurs here and it is this: If the leg bar is to take off for dancing and other active movements then the strings can hang a little loosely, but if the bar is for rocking, or for walking only, then the strings must be just tight enough to hang straight when the puppet is upright, and yet so that the slightest movement of the bar will make a forward movement to the leg thus affected.

Head, shoulder and leg strings are now accounted for; there remain the back and the hands for consideration. In the case of the back, some experts like to have this string fixed to the end of the peg already spoken of as the shoulder peg. The string starts here and finishes at a point in the centre of the back just above waist line (*Figure 55*). Other manipulators make their back string to hang a trifle loosely from a screw-eye at the bottom of the grip rod, but fixed at the same centre waist point on the doll. Personally, the author favours this latter mode, by reason of the fact that the back string is used mainly for the figure to bow, or stoop, an important movement, yet not so often used as the more subtle movements of the head and neck, as when a doll is acting a part in a play for example, and these actions are so much more easily controlled when the shoulder strings are fixed to the end of the shoulder peg than when they hang from the bottom of the grip rod. As it is a somewhat controversial point, the best thing for the operator to do is to experiment for himself by trying the back and shoulder strings from both positions and deciding which method he prefers from his experience.

Finally, the hands. In many cases a simple wire loop or screw-eye fixed in the grip rod

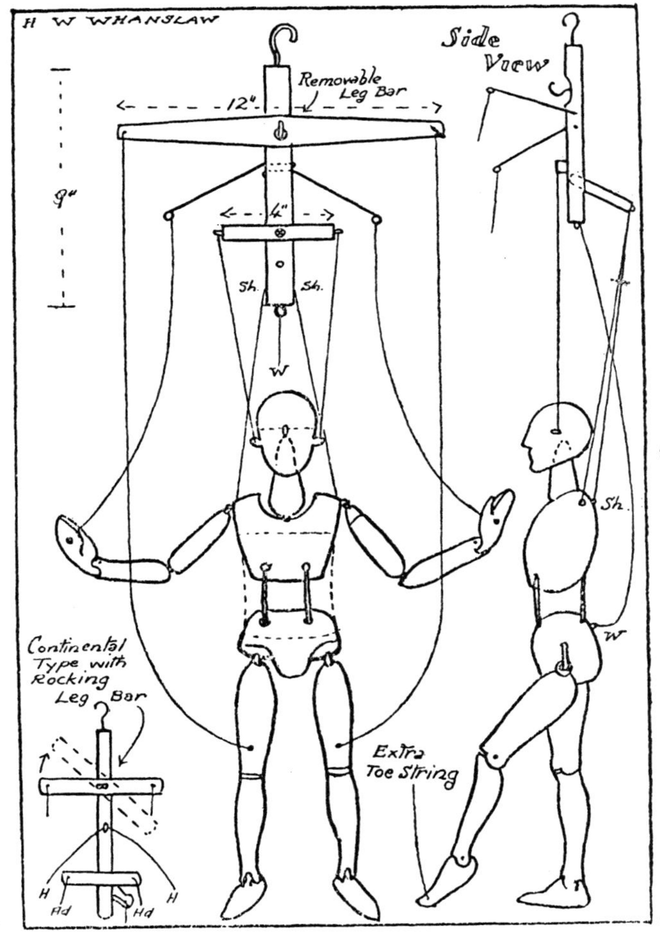

Fig. 55.—Upright control in detail.

just above hand width is used, but a greatly improved hand control is being developed in this country. It originated at the London Marionette Theatre, and at first consisted of a long wire put through a hole in the *side* of the grip, as shown in *Figure* 55, and bent forward into two parallel rods, each about six inches in length, with their ends bent over to form small loops for the string to pass through. The string itself being a run-through thread and hanging just a trifle slack. Later, a single wire with run-through string was used, and another development brought back the second wire, with the difference that now both wires became *separate*, and acting independently of each other, in other words, one wire could move upwards whilst the other rod went downwards, or both come up together. In this case the run-through string was dispensed with, and each hand string was definitely fixed to its corresponding rod (*Figure* 55). In each of the cases mentioned the hand wire was fixed in the *centre* of the hand grip so that it could be manipulated by a simple movement of a finger.

In America very elaborate and complicated controls are made and used. Aluminium instead of wood has been tried, but this seems to make for a certain amount of sound and noise as the metal parts touch each other, which are not part of the programme. The more silent a doll can be when in action the better, even a double screw-eye joint can make a lot of unnecessary sounds and "clicks," which somebody in the audience is going to hear. The Americans favour the aeroplane type, or horizontal control, and have introduced a good many new ideas into the business. They have a kind of lever control for the head which is very good when in action, but as it means a special movement of a finger or hand to operate the lever, the system does not hold a candle to the Continental control, where every movement of the head and neck is made entirely by the wrist, leaving the fingers free for other use.

Some experts like to have the head bar not definitely fixed to the control, but attached to it by means of pieces of strong elastic (*Figure* 56), or springs, another method which also makes for a certain amount of complication, but one which may have great possibilities when the idea has been more fully developed.

So much for the controls. Assuming that the producer has prepared one or more of the perches for his figures, the next business will be to string them up. Here is the point where patience and concentration will need to come well into the limelight. Each string will require to be either *exactly* tight or *exactly* loose, according to its duty and position. Get one head or shoulder string a fraction of an inch tighter than its fellow and the *balance* of the doll will be completely lost. Get one hand or leg string a shade too loose, and instead of an easy movement of the control an extra effort will have to be made to get the limb to answer to the call. So that stringing needs very great care, and all the strings must be accurately adjusted before the puppet will be fit to make its debut in a proper manner.

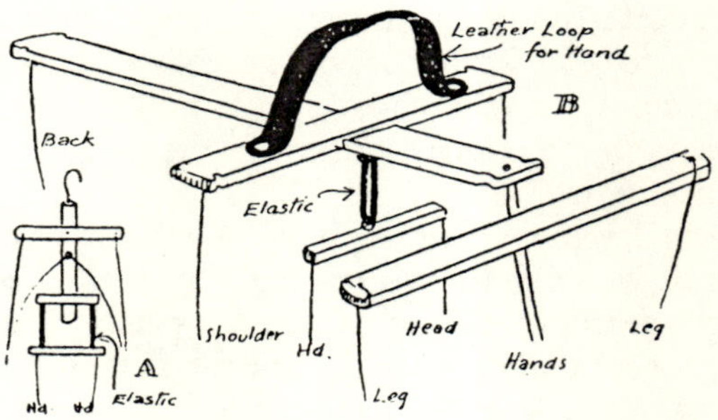

Fig. 56.—With elastic head controls.
(*a*) German. (*b*) American.

A considerable amount of time can be saved and a lot of trouble avoided by having some sort of fixture, a bar or a large hook, from which the control can hang and which is placed a definite and permanent height from the floor, so that when the doll is finally strung its control hook is hanging on this bar or hook, and the feet of the figure rest secure and flat on the floor level, and every string that should be taut is dead tight.

The *positions* of the strings have been indicated already in the various diagrams of controls, and when fixing them it is the best plan to fix the shoulders and head strings first and get them properly adjusted, for on these strings the figure actually depends, and once they are fixed they take the full weight of the doll and make the rest of the task a very simple matter.

The *length* of the strings will depend entirely on the judgment of the puppeteer. If the floor on which the operator stands is on the same level as the stage floor itself, the bridge over which the operator works will be about three feet or three feet six inches high, and the strings of the dolls made according to that height. If, on the other hand, the dolls are to be worked from a high bridge, as in the case of very large marionettes, "three-foot" dolls or larger, the strings will of necessity be long in proportion and additionally strong too.

There are no hard and fast rules on this all-important detail, the chief point to observe is that *all* strings must be considerably longer than the height of the proscenium opening, to prevent the front rows of the audience from seeing the hands of the operators during a performance.

CHAPTER XI

Trick Dolls

APART from the "straight" or normal types of marionettes, the actors in the plays, and general characters, there are certain specialised puppets which will come across the path of the producer from time to time, and require a little thought and experiment before they are perfect in action. The speaking doll has been mentioned already, and details of how to make a marionette pick up a letter or lift up pots and things, are illustrated in *The Bankside Book of Puppets*, but the dolls now to be described, are often to be met with in stock troupes and traditional programmes, and it is just as well to know a thing or two about them.

The Skeleton. This is the character which comes to pieces and joins up again. It is illustrated in *Figure* 57 and will be seen to consist of a series of threadings through loops, a bead like arrangement. Two people can work this doll much better than a single operator, but all that has to be done is to pull the leg bar or foot bar well away and to let the figure slide down the string. It will then come apart and the reverse action will bring it together again. Of course, a great deal of practice will be required on the part of the operator to perfect the movements, but once the doll is "mastered" it is, invariably, a

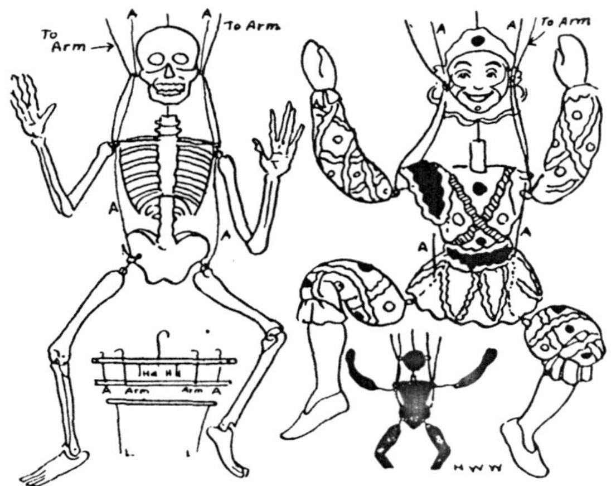

Fig. 57.—Dissecting dolls. The traditional skeleton, and a clown from the Clunn Lewis Troupe now in the collection of C. H. Nicholson, Esq. (*a*) shows the head, body, and leg strings. The arms were controlled by separate strings which passed through the head and shoulder loops.

tremendous success. Other characters may be treated in the same manner. Mr. C. H. Nicholson has in his collection, a clown of the Grimaldi type, purchased from the famous old showman, Clunn Lewis, and this figure does the very same disintegration trick.

Another and entirely different marionette is shown in the puppet known as "Oopsie,"

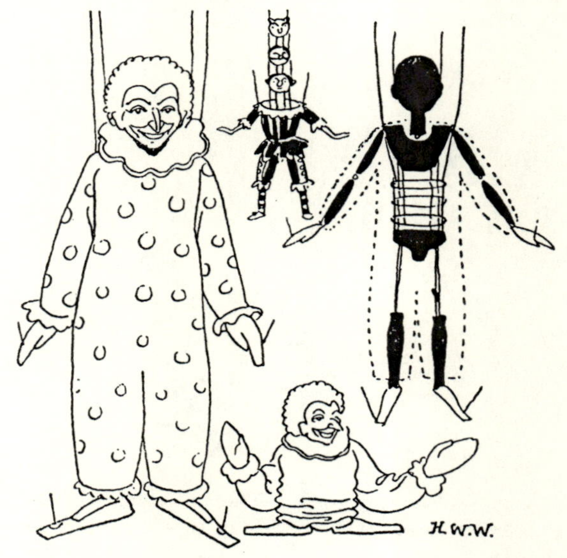

Fig. 58.—The collapsing doll "Oopsie" of the Rozella Troupe, and the three-headed "Scaramouche" of the same troupe.

which was originally a member of the Rozella troupe. This is one of the extending types of doll, and consists of a solid head, hands and feet, but neither body, arms, nor legs, only a costume connecting the existing parts. This figure can be made to come out of a pot, like "Jack-in-the-Box," and to do an extraordinary selection of extremely funny actions. A further variety of this class of trick figure is seen in the "Scaramouche," which has three heads, one above the other, all of which are tucked into

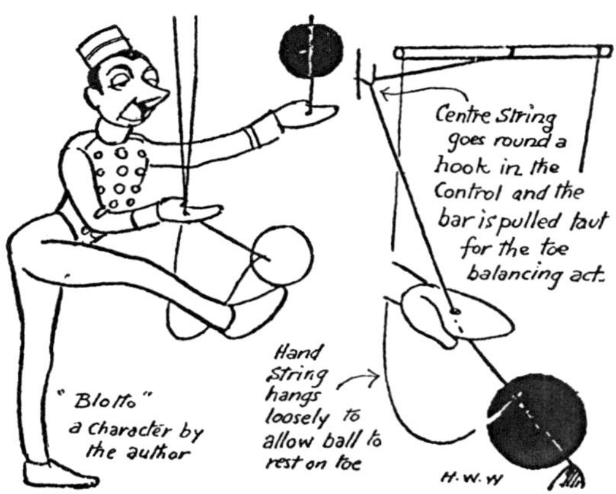

Fig. 59.—Juggling and toe balancing.

his body and are made to appear in a gradual sequence (*Figure* 58).

Then there are puppets which *juggle* with balls and other objects. The balls are large, wooden beads and are threaded through hand strings, and special strings to the feet, as illustrated in the picture of "Blotto," the comic page boy of the London Marionette Theatre. Making a doll lift up a bottle to its mouth, smell a bunch of flowers, or play a mouth organ is done by a string from the hand which passes through the mouth and out

Fig. 60.—Trick actions, playing musical instruments, smelling flowers, raising hats, bowing, etc.

at the top of the head. There are an endless variety of movements of this description, and they are some of the simplest of trick actions that can be done. On the same principle, marionettes can be made to put their hands to their hearts, or play guitars, banjos or other instruments of a like nature, because the control string for this action passes through a screw-eye or metal loop fixed into the chest or on the top of the guitar, as the case may be.

Trapeze Artists may have special strings from the hands which pass through the bar of

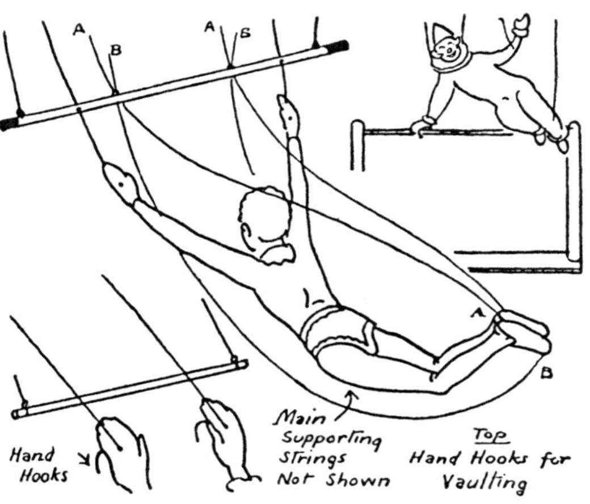

Fig. 61.—Fixed trapeze figure and hand hooks.

the trapeze or rope as in the case of the famous "Bil-bal-bull" of the Teatro dei Piccoli, or they can have a little metal hook in each hand by which they clutch the horizontal bar or trapeze, and the manipulator can then pull on a pair of strings specially attached to the feet, and so make the acrobat stand on his hands, a trick which never fails to give a lot of pleasure, like "Mister Henery Mobbs," the strong-man acrobat of the Hogarth Puppets, by Jan Bossell.

Smoking Dolls have long narrow tubing fitted into the bodies and up to the mouth.

Fig. 62.—Smoking and other trick actions.

This tubing is carried "off" stage, and the smoke is blown through by an assistant.

Most marionette tricks are produced by one or other of the methods described and illustrated. If the craftsman is an ingenious sort of person, he will discover means of making marionettes do what appears to the audience as being most marvellous things. They will stand on their heads, they will jump through hoops (apparently), they will change into other beings as though some puppet witch had cast a spell upon them. They will turn the pages of the music they are playing on the piano in the manner of the Italian maestro of the Vittorio Podrecca Troupe, or like " Faust " in the Ivo Puhonny production of that famous drama. All these things will they do, and much more besides. One thing, however, the producer should remember, a sort of *Golden Rule*, never to be forgotten, and that is *never to repeat a trick* more than once after a puppet has successfully accomplished it. This means that trick dolls will occupy the stage for only very short spells and this is good, because the longer the audience remain mystified and the thing is above their heads the greater the success of the wonderful marionette is going to be.

In the production of a straight play there are seldom opportunities for trick dolls in the true sense of the word, but none the more for that, there are often occasions, even in the most serious of dramas, where a little bit of trick controlling and manipulation are required; picking up letters, hats and so on. In such a case as this the craftsman or operator must seek to make the action a perfectly natural one, without any show or preliminary jiggery to attract the attention of the audience so that they might all "get" the wonderful trick to its best advantage. In a play the puppets are actors; they *are* the people they represent, and every action they do must be as nearly normal and reasonable as good manipulation will allow it to be.

CHAPTER XII

THE MARIONETTE IN ACTION

WHEN the dolls are *not* in use they must be covered with bags or tie-on sleeves and hung upon a rod out of the way of the performers. When they *are* being used in a show they should be hung up in a similar manner on a rod or strong rope placed conveniently near the stage; *then* the operator can put up a doll as it comes off the stage and reach for another to make its entry, without having to walk about too much to get at them. If the stage is of the portable, rectangular-frame type described in an earlier part of this book, it will have a series of rods fitted for this purpose. It is *most important* that *all* marionettes to be used during a performance should be ready to hand, in order that delays of entry may be eliminated or at least brought down to a minimum of time.

This means that the rod or rope must be securely fixed, the rope in particular very tightly stretched so as not to sag in the middle when the combined weight of a number of dolls get on it. Also it means that the hook on top of each control must be large enough to go over the bar or rope with ease. Little things like this, if carefully attended to will go far towards assisting in the smooth running of the whole show. If possible the rod should be hung at a height within easy reach of the operator or his assistant's hands—standing on a box or a chair to reach down a doll may

Fig. 63.—Making an entry with the marionette already in action.

mean an unexpected crash or tumble, an even which can quite easily put a whole show out o action.

When a doll makes an entry it should com in *on the stage level* as if it had *walked few steps* before being actually "on"; no "floated" down from the "flies" as thoug it was just landing from a parachute descent. Real, human actors walk on to the stage and what is more, they start to act *before* they are "on," so that their entry may appear perfectly natural. Therefore marionettes must make *their* entries in exactly the same way (*Figure* 63). These remarks apply to their *exits* also; to "yank" a doll straight up into the air as soon as it reaches the wings *may* save time, but it will lose his reputation for the operator if ever the audience see him doing it. The puppet can walk, or dance, or spring off, but it must never be swished off as though it was being taken up by a whirlwind.

As soon as a puppet is "on" it is in action. It ceases to be a doll and becomes, in the master's hands, a *being*, a personality interpreting by its movements the mind of the operator and the character he wishes it to be. And all this time, from the moment of its entry to that of its exit, the operator must concentrate the whole of his attention on the little man at the end of the strings; especially if the operator is speaking the puppet's part in the play as well as controlling its actions. Should the master's attention be diverted or should his thoughts wander for but a single moment there will be trouble, for the continuity is broken; the mental thread that makes the puppet and his master an entity is snapped. The effect of this lapse may be disastrous.

The other operators on the bridge, keyed up tc their cues, trained to act with machine-like precision in unison one with the other, will lose contact with *their* puppets also, and their holc on their dolls will slacken and cause them tc lose their character at once.

In a speaking play particularly, ever}

Fig. 64.—Rehearsing with the aid of a looking glass.

operator has to be ready for the unexpecte(emergency, from a broken string to a droppe(leg bar, ready to concentrate on his own par to keep the continuity going and to absolutel *ignore* that broken thread, or whatever it ma be, as though it had never taken place at all.

A player may forget his lines, any littl

distraction behind the stage or in front of it can make him do this, and if he cannot remember the exact words of his lines he must say something that as nearly as possible means the same thing as the forgotten phrase, so that his partner can take up the thread of the actual play in his reply, and should an operator get hopelessly stuck, " dried up," then his partners will need to use all their ready wits to keep the talk and action alive until the general equilibrium is restored.

Of course, there will be a copy of the play fixed to a stand or reading board on the back of the proscenium and its pages turned over by a player as the drama proceeds. Some experts think this an entirely unnecessary help, and advocate that the operators should know their lines so thoroughly and be so well rehearsed that a prompter alone will be all that is wanted in an emergency. But the average small travelling show will not be able to afford to carry around an extra person in the form of a prompter—a two-handed show, for example—and that's where the reading desk and the open manuscript is going to do its part. If the operators are good at their job they will very soon learn the words and their actions will automatically synchronise with the words of the play. This form of dramatic art is very different from that of the human actor, in that the operator has a complicated mass of threads under his control, in addition to remembering and speaking his lines in the play, so that it is all the more essential for him to get his "talk" well memorised in order to speed up the synchronisation of speech and action. At the same time it is a considerable help to the

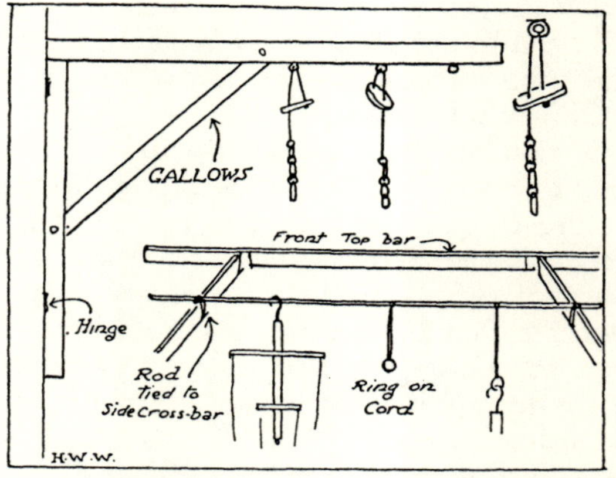

Fig. 65.—Methods of hanging crowds and additional marionettes on the stage for action.

operator to know that his book of words is open before him in case of an emergency.

And these emergencies can and will happen, make no mistake about that, strings of a doll making an entry will get caught on some trifling little thing, even a splinter too small almost, to be seen by the eye of the keyed-up manipulator, will catch a string and cause a most heart-breaking moment of anxiety to blight the operator's mood. Sometimes a doll can be " on " before one loose string, which has caught on a snag, will drag and pull the figure right out of action. All kinds of things seem to conspire against the manipulator, and a very careful watch must be kept on the strings at every entry and exit, so that even when there are no words of a play to be spoken the operator will need to have all his wits about him, but in the case of a play it is easy to see how any small outside cause like this can throw the operator off his lines.

Another important point. All outside *sounds* must be reduced to a minimum if not entirely eliminated. The floor of the stage or bridge on which the manipulator stands should be covered with felt or carpet. Failing this, the operators must wear slippers or rubber soled shoes. Conversation must cease save for necessary instructions which must be given in whispers or by signs. The wearing of wrist watches should be avoided as the little, milled winding screw has a nasty habit of catching into strings. So, also, do buttons on sleeves and details of a like nature.

All properties should be in charge of one responsible assistant—*the property master*—whose duty it is to see that these important scenic units are not only placed on the stage at the right moment and removed from thence when the scene is finished, *but also* that all properties are kept together in a definite place behind the stage and not allowed to litter the floor in a dangerous and unseemly manner. When a doll or detail comes off the stage it must go back to the place from whence it came—and nowhere else.

All movements must be done in *silence*. It should be as quiet behind the proscenium as in the auditorium. The staff must treat the whole thing seriously while a performance is in progress and not as a pastime. Try to organise the thing into a routine which becomes almost automatic, with the operators going about their business quietly and systematically, everything in its proper place and every detail ready for its proper entry.

Performances should start as nearly as possible to the tick of the clock; this means that everything must be ready beforehand and all operators and assistants standing by at their posts, all dolls in place and everything overhauled by those in charge. If a gramophone or panatrope is used for the music, all records must be arranged in their respective order, and a separate place kept ready to receive the used records as they come off the instrument, so that they will not get mixed up with those yet to be used, incidentally, it is a good plan to stick a label on each record the side that is to be used, with a good-sized number on it indicating its place in the programme.

If a record case is used or an album, the discs should be put back into it as they are used. Records are valuable and, in most cases, very hard to replace; so that great care

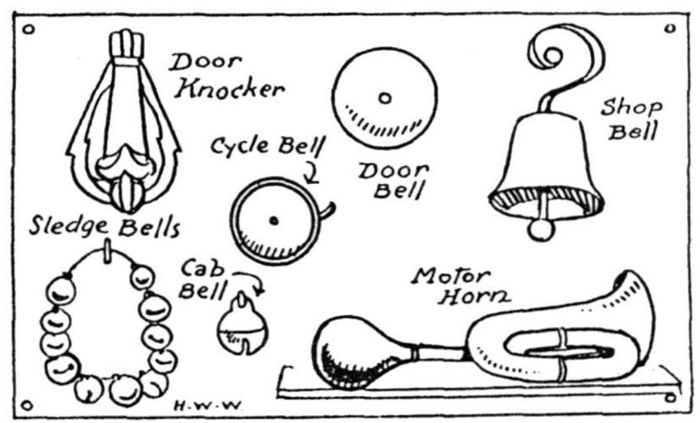

Fig. 66.—Suggestions for an "effects" board. All kinds of noise effects can be grouped on a board in this manner.

must be taken in their handling in order that their lives may be preserved as long as possible. This, of course, is a job for the musical director, and right at the beginning of the whole business it will be well to allocate different jobs to the various operators and for each to *keep strictly* to his or her job, and to refrain from attempting to do some other person's job as well, even if they do think said person is not doing it so well as they themselves feel capable of doing it.

With everybody dodging about behind the stage and all trying to do the same thing at once there will be nothing but confusion and delay—and the second evil is worse than the first. While this matter of jobs for all is under consideration let the author add one brief bit of advice to whoever is in charge of the whole business, the puppet master, the producer, the owner of the troupe, or whatever he likes to call himself, and that is to put all your *confidence in your assistants* and to let them *know* that you trust them—don't snatch things out of their hands and do whatever they were going to do yourself, as though *you* were the only capable person in the troupe. If a mistake or accident occurs, treat it *as a mistake* or accident and not as a *fault*, and finally, get a good idea of the value of a pat on the back: a little praise can go a long way, and if everybody in the troupe realises that if there are any honours to be shared *they* will share it as well as the head of the troupe, then your assistants will have confidence in *you*, which is even more important than your confidence in them. It is a tremendous asset to a troupe to have absolute agreement and confidence between all parties concerned, with everybody doing their own particular job to the best of their ability, and nobody monopolising the limelight when the time for giving praise and credit comes round.

If printed programmes are used, see that the names of:—(1) The designers and makers of each doll is given, if possible. (2) The name of every assistant and person definitely attached to the troupe are printed on it. Little details like this go a tremendous way towards making the troupe a jolly little community.

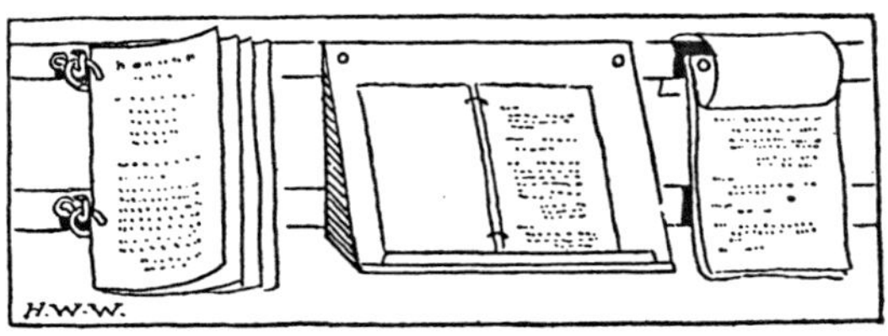

Fig. 67.—Methods of arranging play MS. for operators.

Some managers like to invite the audience around after a performance to show off the dolls and also to keep the interest going. If the show is good the audience will go home and tell their friends about it and how it was done. Sometimes this invitation to a " look round " leads to " bookings." Sometimes it encourages some enterprising individuals to start in and make a troupe for themselves, introducing some of the tricks you have been so kind as to explain to them, and which took you so long to produce and bring to perfection.

This business of allowing visitors to the back of the stage is really a personal matter for each producer to decide alone, but there is one big thing to be said *against* it, and that is the danger of unskilled persons handling the dolls at a moment when the attention of those in charge is taken up by another enchanted visitor asking " how is it done." The writer has vivid memories of cases of this description, and of one in particular when a perfectly innocent and well-meaning lady picked up a puppet to examine its costume, and *her* attention being taken off by conversation, she turned the doll upside down and allowed it to somersault into its own strings, and any puppet operator who has tried to disentangle a marionette that has done a thing like this will understand the writer's emotions when he had to watch this accident, but was unable to get near enough to prevent it happening because of the rest of a crowd of visitors milling around.

CHAPTER XIII

THE GLOVE PUPPET

IN the sleeve doll, or glove puppet, one has, probably, the oldest form of puppet entertainment known to man. Certainly the earliest picture of a puppet show illustrates the sleeve doll in action. That picture is a miniature by Jehan de Grise, it was painted sometime between the years 1338 and 1344 on a manuscript entitled, " Li Romans du Bon Roi Alixandre " and is in the Bodleian Library at Oxford.

In Italy the sleeve dolls are known as " Burattini," and they are to be found in various forms in many countries. In Germany and neighbouring countries the theatre is called a *Kasperle* Theatre, in England we call it a " Punch and Judy Show."

In that wonderful book " Dolls and Puppets," by Max Von Boehn, which has been translated into English by Mrs. Josephine Nicoll,* a very complete description is given of the history of these shows; space is much too limited to give even the very briefest of stories here, and as this book deals with the practical

* *See* Bibliography at the end of this book.

side of the business, the reader is recommended to refer to one or other of the books mentioned in the bibliography for further details.

In all cases, and in every period, the method of performing with these dolls was much about the same. The *theatre* consisted of a three or four sided framework, surrounded by canvas or

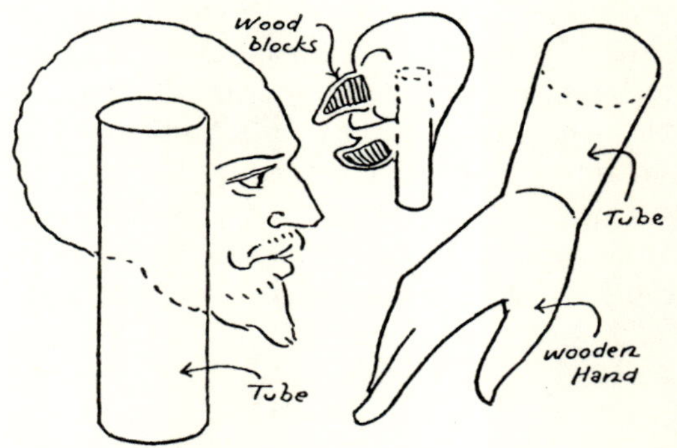

Fig. 68.—Heads and hand for glove puppets.

linen, and with a proscenium opening in front a foot or so higher than the height of the operator. Sometimes the back was left open, exposing the manipulator to the full view of passers by, but in the majority of cases the framework was screened all around. Along the base of the proscenium opening was a shelf about six inches wide, this formed the play-board, the "stage" upon which all the properties were rested and the action took place.

In some of the old prints of street puppet shows there is a little slit or opening in the front of the cloth surround, just below the proscenium, out of which Punch or Kasperl, as the case may be, would poke his head from time to time. A lot of operators do this with their puppets, and it was evidently a practice with the operators to make their dolls hold conversation with the audience a century or so ago, just as the modern Punch and Judy showman does to-day.

The showman who proposes to travel with a sleeve doll outfit would first of all require some dolls, because a great amount of work could be done even without a booth to play in. Curtains stretched across an opening with a piece of drapery as a back cloth, will give the same effect as a built theatre would present. A doorway between two rooms, a draped clothes horse on a kitchen table and many other ways of making a temporary theatre would occur to a person of ingenuity. The audience will forget the structure of the stage as soon as action begins.

Therefore, make some dolls first of all and get your "hands in," in both senses of the word. The *heads* will be carved in *light-weight* wood or modelled in papier mâché, after the manner described in the chapter on "Heads." For lightness in weight the papier mâché variety is to be preferred. The features should be exaggerated, prominent noses, and incidentally, if the character is to be a "knock-about" with a lot of head play, it will be a good plan to fill *the nose* of the

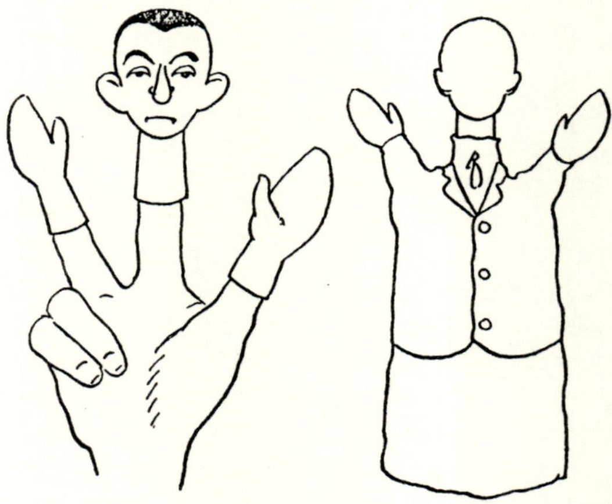

Fig. 69.—Manipulation. How the glove puppets are held and dressed.

mâché figure with a piece of wood. Prominent eyebrows and very definite expressions are essential also. The neck will be a hollow tube of sufficient diameter to take the index finger of the hand. Very clever heads in plastic wood and also in papier mâché are made by Colin A. Gray, of the Bura Puppets. These are extremely light in weight but tremendously strong. The character in each head is very pronounced, some of the heads almost bordering on the grotesque, but very full of expression when in action.

Papier mâché heads are used by the "Modicot Shpeel Puppets," the famous Yiddish Marionette Theatre of New York. and by many of the Continental operators. *Figure* 69 shows the construction of a glove doll head and also the *hands*, which have tubular wrists to take the thumb and second finger of the hand. The method of holding the dolls is also illustrated.

The clothes are made to fit around these tubes and form the sleeve into which the operator puts his arm. At the base of each figure is a small *metal ring* by which it is hooked in position below the proscenium ready for its cue.

In the illustration of the manipulator at work it will be seen at once, why light-weight figures are to be recommended. The effort of holding the arms above the head for any sustained period would be even more difficult if a pair of very heavy dolls were being supported. In the Italian Burratini Theatres the operator sits down on a stool and rests his elbows on a special shelf placed in a convenient position. This relieves the strain to a considerable degree. The French "Guignol" dolls which have very large wooden heads are some of the heaviest of this type of puppets to handle.

The actual amount of movement obtainable by the sleeve doll is, of course, limited, but after a certain amount of practice the operator

Fig. 70.—Methods of manipulation. In the right-hand corner is shown the use of the pocket, or opening in the proscenium below the play board.

will find that he can *suggest* a great deal of action. Bowing, dancing, walking and sitting are very simple actions, but with the fingers controlling the hands the puppets may be made to pick up things and even throw articles about. Mr. Walter Wilkinson, probably the greatest of English operators of glove dolls, makes one of his characters actually plane a block of wood. His dolls throw things to one another and catch them. T. Maynard Parker, another great manipulator, makes a character take a match from a box held by another figure and strike it, and when a dude tries to snatch a kiss from a passing girl the lady changes into a man, when "her" mask and hair disappear.

A useful fitting is a trick hand which is made on the principle of the spring clothes peg, in fact, some operators use an actual peg for the job. With a hand of this description the picking up and holding of properties is made an easy matter.

In the *Catalan*, or Spanish type of puppet, the figure has much longer arm tubes, and *three* fingers are used for the head, which has shoulders and breast, instead of only one (*Figure* 71).

On many of the Continental dolls, legs are fitted as well as arms, much the same as on the English Punch, which enables him to sit on the playboard with his legs dangling in front of the audience. The dolls with legs usually have a *black* sleeve at the back for the operator's arm to go up into the body, *Figure* 71 illustrates this type of puppet.

The *fit-up* for this work is, as already

mentioned, a simple screen-like set of frames. The height of the playboard above the ground is somewhere about five feet six inches and the top of the proscenium opening about two feet above this. Some showmen like to have a

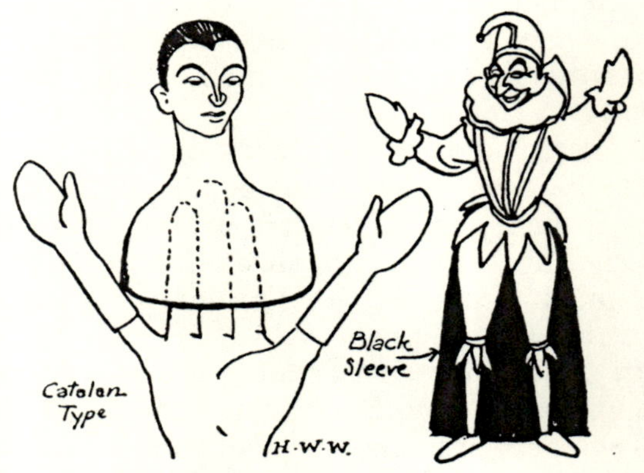

Fig. 71.—Details of the Catalan type of doll and a glove puppet with legs showing the black sleeve for the manipulator's arm.

small " room " and window on either side of the proscenium, out of which characters poke their heads and various comic actions take place (*Figure* 70).

Maynard Parker's stage, which is typical of

this kind of fit-up, is in the form of a shallow box with two hinged extending sides. It is fitted with an additional shelf below the play-board for properties and incidentals. This shelf is fitted with a row of hooks upon which the dolls hang inverted, ready for the operator to plunge his hands into their bags, lift them off and into action in one quick movement. The puppets hang as the illustration shows, always ready for their cue, each character on its own particular hook, to which it returns immediately it comes " off."

The stage is fitted with a black gauze screen behind which the operator works and through which he can *see* his audience, but the audience cannot see him. Mr. Parker works with a slightly lower proscenium level than is usual in this type of show and thus is enabled to stand and see through the gauze screen. In the use of a screen like this, great care has to be taken to see that *no light* comes in from the *back*, otherwise the operator himself will be seen too.

Scenery is of the simplest type. Back cloths which are held in position by a bar resting on the top of the fit-up frame, side pieces and units which can be made to hook quickly and easily on to the upright post each side of the proscenium.

The *width* of the proscenium opening will be a matter of personal taste on the part of the showman, and also the business of portability will have to be taken into consideration. The French Guignol Theatres have wide openings and, in a general way, a wide opening is to be preferred, as a scene appears a great deal more spacious, and comic battle scenes can take on so much more speed and energy if the operator has plenty of room in which to perform. A tall, narrow show gives a "boxed in" appearance, besides giving the operator a cramped space in which to move about.

Lighting is obtained from a shaded lamp or row of lamps held in front of the theatre by brackets and tilted to an angle of about forty-five degrees. The glove theatre differs from the larger marionette stage in that its lighting system is a much more simple affair. A tri-colour system could be arranged in the front batten if desired, but this would mean a special switch board and more work for the operator, who already has both hands well filled, and as this is essentially a "one-man show" the simplest methods are the most practicable. The operator will find that all his attention is occupied with his play, and that while a show is on, it is a full-time business.

Toy musical instruments are used by many workers to give sound effects. Mouth organs, jazzophones, whistles and a hundred and one things of this description are brought into action. Things like mouth organs should be

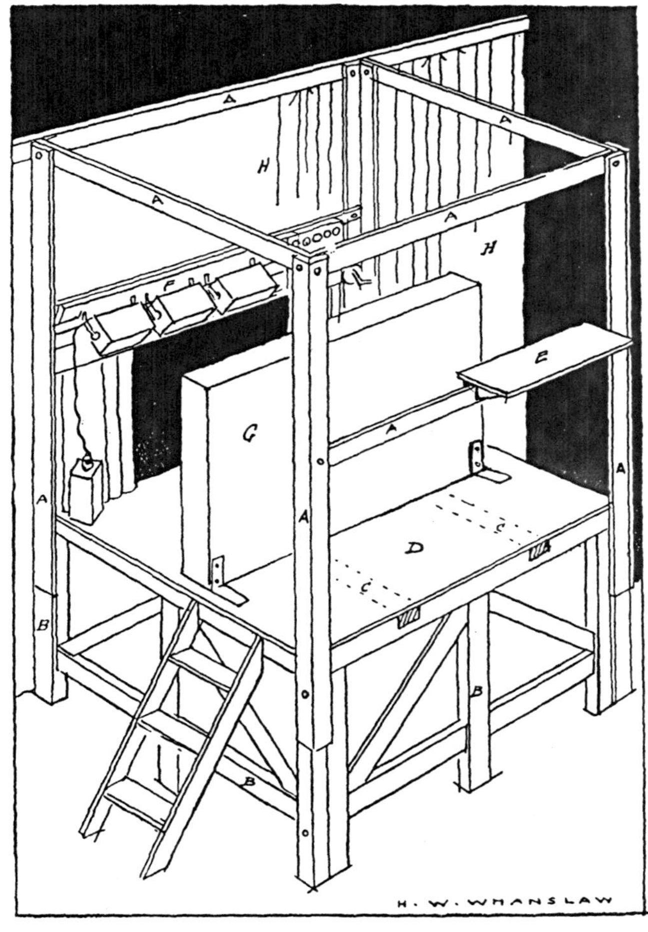

Fig. 72.—The fit-up for glove puppets.

firmly fixed in some spot well within reach of the operator's mouth, in order that they can be played *whilst* he is using both arms to hold up his puppets.

A very interesting experiment was tried by Mr. Maynard Parker, who made a puppet stage intended for use without a proscenium. It is illustrated in *Figure* 73, and when action was taking place the puppets came up *inside* the towers on either side, through the doors on to the stage. The windows suggested rooms like the side panel windows in an ordinary show. In appearance the fit-up looked mediæval and suggested the production of old-time plays done in a perfectly serious manner. This "castello" type has been tried out by other great operators. William Simmonds, most famous of all English marionette producers, built a somewhat similar set for sleeve dolls which was exhibited at the International Exhibition of the Art of the Theatre at South Kensington.

This took the form of a Norman castle with windows and entrances, and the puppets represented knights, ladies, heralds and characters of a description usually found in such a place.

To-day there are a number of most excellent operators, apart from the men already mentioned. Each of these men is a specialist, doing an entirely different performance to anyone else. Wallace Peat, of Bristol, has made a name for himself with his interpretations of Old English Folk Songs and Shakespearean productions. P. F. Tickner does the good old drama of "Mr. Punch" in a way that few of the old street showmen have ever succeeded in "putting it over," and there are many other

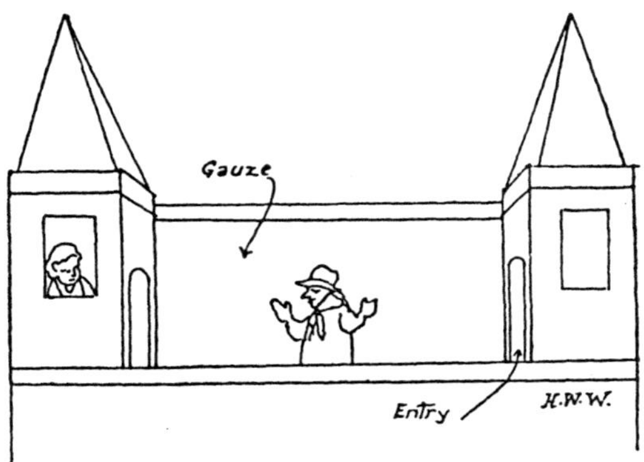

Fig. 73.—The Maynard-Parker Castello.

operators like Chas. H. Nicholson, members of the British Puppet and Model Theatre Guild, who are capable of doing a first-class show and holding their audience to the very last minute. Most of these people make their own figures.

In schools the art is being taken up because

of its value in the teaching of handwork, and also because dolls of this description can be constructed very easily and from all kinds of waste materials.

Heads and hands can be made of stockinette or velvet, with beads for eyes, and many other suggestions will occur to the teacher once the class has made a start with the work. Miniature shows of this description, with soft dolls, can be constructed for bed ridden children in hospitals and similar institutions.

Animals form a very interesting part of the troupe. No show is complete without its crocodile or its dragon and, if the producer has an inventive mind, many weird and wonderful beasts can be made.

The old-time Punch showman, as well as his modern confrères, used a tiny squeaker, known in the business as a "call." The piercing squeals of Mr. Punch could be heard from a long way off, but the general practice of using a thing of this description is not recommended, as the squeakers themselves are so small that it is a perfectly easy matter to swallow one.

The first man to perform his Punch show in the streets of London was an Italian named Porsini. Rumour tells that he was preceded by a woman operator, but no actual record of this is to be seen. Porsini was the great man of his time—the end of the eighteenth century—and all the honour and glory goes to his name. But the man who followed him did a lot to endear his name with every child—and grown-up for that matter—who has looked upon a Punch show since his day. His name was Pike, and he was the first man to use a real, live Toby dog in his show.

CHAPTER XIV

PRODUCTIONS

THE choice of shows must be left entirely to the will and pleasure of the producer. If he is a wise man he will give consideration to suggestions that are bound to be made by interested visitors and members of his audiences. Sometimes a very helpful idea may come through such a channel as this, though in very many cases the suggestions so freely given by outsiders are either useless or impracticable, for the simple reason that nine times out of ten the would-be helper has no practical knowledge of the technical side of producing a marionette play and either suggests a thing requiring most intricate and elaborate scenic effects, or one in which too many dolls are required, or too many changes of costume, which means duplicate figures and, perhaps, impossible movements and actions on the stage. In any case, it is well to have a few variety turns " up your sleeve," in reserve, because even if your ambition is to do serious dramas or plays of any description, in all cases these plays *must* be short. Too long duration can weary an audience just as constant repetition of a puppet's tricks will do the same thing.

Therefore, let the plays be short, " snappy " as the Americans say. If possible, have something jolly in the programme: " One man's meat is another man's poison," and ninety-nine out of every hundred audiences comprise people of every mood, so that even if you do an all-serious drama, have a heart for the other people in the auditorium who enjoy a laugh, and put on some bright, cheerful stuff for these, *because* both types of onlookers will go home and tell their friends about your show, and if everybody says it was good the value of your show as an entertainment will increase a hundredfold.

Let every act or variety turn be *complete*, in that it ends with a " finish." It must contain and exhibit a definite idea, and not consist merely of dolls jigging and wandering aimlessly about the stage. Let *every* puppet *do something*. In the great show of the " Teatro dei Piccoli," Dr. Podrecca's wonderful troupe of Italian marionettes, there were dolls who could cross their legs or pick up things, could do certain intricate dancing steps, and one priceless character who could take off his coat. They *did things*, and in consequence were successful marionettes and held their audiences. However beautifully made a marionette may be, if it is useless, it *is* useless.

Duplicated dolls have been mentioned. This is the best way in which to make a character come on again in a new dress. To play about behind trying to fit fresh dresses on dolls is not only bad business, but also a very difficult thing to do with any sort of success, especially if the change has to be a quick one.

Music

Here is another important branch of the work. Some producers like to use instruments, pipes, tabor, or tambourine, violins and piano. This is excellent, it is surprising what exquisite music can be obtained from a quartet of pipes, or a trio of piano, violin and 'cello. If it be possible, something like this is by far and away the best type of music for a first-class show. There are a great many people even to-day who dislike what they are pleased to call "tinned music," and sometimes when one hears an ancient record being played on a none-too-good gramophone, one feels very much inclined to agree with them.

At the same time a gramophone is an extremely useful instrument, especially for use with a portable show. With a good machine, a good sound-box, and good records, some very fine music can be obtained.

Just at present, however, the playing of the majority of gramophone records in public has to be paid for. A year or so ago one could buy and play almost any record to almost any audience without fee or licence, but since the formation of Phonographic Industries, Ltd., the playing of records in public can be done only on payment of a fee. What that fee is depends entirely on the nature and number of performances one is going to produce; so, for those producers who wish to use records made by any of the firms in the Association, the best thing to do is to get in touch with the Secretary and explain matters so that an arrangement can be made and an agreement entered into right from the start. This will save a great deal of worry and also eliminate the possibility of undesirable legal complications.

There is on the market another make of record which is in no way connected with the big Association of record makers. These records are known as "Octacros Records," and for the public performance of these no licence fees, other than those of the Performing Rights Society, are required. They are made by the Synchrophone Company, and a very large and varied selection of tunes and subjects can be obtained.

Apart from the stock records made by the various companies, it is now possible to have records made privately and exclusively to suit a producer's especial needs. These are called "Permarec" records and are supplied by

Musikon, Ltd., of Lisle Street, W.C. 2. They can be made in ten-inch, twelve-inch and also in sixteen-inch discs, and are produced in a specially fitted studio, entirely sound proof. The records have a metal basis covered with the substance in which the recording grooves are cut.

From the same source may be obtained an outfit for recording music and speech in one's own home. An extremely useful thing, especially for making permanent, *unbreakable* records of an exclusive production.

In all cases, *apart from privately owned* and made records, such as the "Permarec," the person in charge of the musical side of the show should make sure of all these details, such as licences, fees and other incidentals, before any *public* shows are given. By a public performance is meant a show taking place in a hall or other place where the public are admitted either by programme or ticket, or payment of any kind. Private performances are not affected by these things. It will be well for the director to get into touch with the Performing Rights Society and any other Association likely to be affected by the show.

Another thing to make sure about when looking for a hall is that it conforms with all the rules and regulations laid down by the authorities, for ensuring the safety of the public. Properly arranged exits in case of fire, doors to open *outwards*, not inwards, good ventilation and other safety devices.

Also that the seating arrangements are in good order and, if they are in tiers, that the foundations of these seats are strong, secure, and not likely to collapse under the weight of the audience. There are a whole lot of things to be considered before the doors can be flung open and the long, long queue a-winding down the street, be allowed to rush in. But once they are well and truly done, and everything is satisfactory as far as AUTHORITY is concerned, the producer can get on with his real job in confidence, knowing that there is need for neither fear nor reproach.

Marionettes as an Advertising Medium

Modern advertising methods have opened up a new field for the marionette. As a form of attraction and a means of giving visual information about a product a marionette performance is a most excellent thing. The author writes from personal experience, for the London Marionette Theatre has done this thing for several well-known products, in large stores in places like Southsea, Exeter, Cardiff, Swansea, Nottingham, Newcastle, Scarborough and Hull, which have been visited with outstanding success. In Cardiff alone over twelve hundred people saw performances in *one day*, and this means that a very great percentage of these people have received mental impressions that will never be effaced, and coupled with the memory of the show is a memory of the product which provided the show.

The fit-up described in this book is the

Fig. 74.—A scene in the first television broadcast of marionettes.

actual theatre used on many of these occasions, and it was found that it was adaptable to every store in which the show was performed. The plain, draped front harmonising in every way with the permanent decorations and fittings of the store.

The marionettes should not be less than eighteen to twenty inches in height, if it is to be used in large emporiums, but it seems that there is a field for a smaller, one-man-show kind of fit-up that would be suitable for stores and shops where space is limited. For a theatre of this description, absolute refinement of taste should be aimed at. Anything coarse or inartistic should be avoided like the plague. Have the dolls well made and well dressed, the scenery good, the music bright and jolly, and the audience will go away happy, and some of them will make it their business to compliment the manager of the store on his attraction, and this means that the travellers of the firm you represent will hear about the great success, and report the same to headquarters when next they write.

On tours of this nature the first thing to do is to sink one's own identity and take on the name of your firm or product. While shows are proceeding you are a part of the firm who is paying your wages and it will all go down as good marks in your favour if the people whom you represent find that a big rush of business results from wherever you go.

In some cases special puppets will have to be constructed to represent the commodities to be advertised, with special plays and music to carry the story along and make it attractive. As a rule each performance should be from about twenty to forty minutes' duration, but the shorter shows are to be preferred; more can be done during the day, and bigger crowds attended to.

Marionette advertising is in its infancy. The London Marionette Theatre is practically the pioneer of this branch of the art, but the field is extremely wide and a great deal can yet be done. So far, no one has produced a glove puppet *advertising* show, and it may be that there is a place for this kind of puppet in the branch. It certainly could be done in smaller stores where space is valuable and accommodation limited.

The Cinema

From time to time a film appears on the screen in which puppets play a more or less important part. Sometimes they are but incidental details, introduced to give a certain amount of local colouring, or because a trifling event in the story necessitates their presence. Sometimes, however, they form the main theme of the story, as in the film "I am Suzanne," in which the famous "Teatro dei Piccoli" and the American Yale Puppeteers share the honours.

The Gorno Marionettes were in the process of making marionette films at the time when the disastrous fire in the studios at Wembley destroyed their famous troupe. Undaunted, they began again to make their dolls, they made new characters, including caricatures of famous film stars, and a number of definite marionette films were then produced in which no human beings took part. Other great puppet films like the Starevitch picture " The Magic Clock," and other productions of this master have been placed before the public on various occasions. " News-reels " of marionettes in which the " London Marionettes " have played a conspicuous part have been shown, but no attempt apart from the Gorno films, seems to have been made to do any serious work with them. There is a great field here, as in the case with advertising shows, and with really well made, first-class puppets, finely constructed scenery and properties, added to absolute control of the dolls on the part of the operators, there is every reason to believe that a good film producer could make some wonderful pictures. The shadow films of Lotte Reininger are marvellous productions, exquisite works of art, and why should not beautiful marionette pictures be placed on the screen too ?

Television is another field wherein marionettes have been used. At the Baird Studios in Long Acre, marionettes were projected by the televisor on a number of occasions. In this case the acting area was extremely small, about twelve inches deep by about fifteen wide. The scenery was drawn in extremely bold, heavy lines, particularly the vertical lines, and in black and white. *Red* being a colour that televises very badly, the dolls' faces were "made-up" in white and black as much as possible, and all red parts of the costume were either covered with some more suitable material, or removed and replaced by other colours. An interesting feature of these experiments was the fact that, by means of a marionette, the full length human figure was televised for the first time. *Figure* 74 illustrates some of the dolls that actually appeared on these experimental broadcasts.

Television is young, though even during the short time the author and his partner have been concerned in its operation, tremendous strides have been made and wonderful results achieved. But, from a technical standpoint, there is a lot to be done before the science becomes as universally popular as the cinema or wireless.

BIBLIOGRAPHY

Marionettes

Uniform with this volume

WHANSLAW, H. W.: "Everybody's Theatre.' Deals with the making of a model theatre, marionettes and shadow shows.

"The Bankside Book of Puppets." Instruction in making a table marionette theatre and various forms of marionettes, shadow figures, etc., in a more advanced manner than "Everybody's Theatre." *See also* the Bibliographies in these books.

VON BOEHN, MAX: "Dolls and Puppets." London: George Harrap & Co., Ltd. 1932. Translated into English by Josephine Nicoll.

BUSSELL, JAN and HOGARTH, ANN. "Puppets." Pepler & Sewell, Ditchling, Sussex. A handbook of marionette work.

McISAAC, F. J.: "Marionettes and How to Make Them." London: Stanley Paul & Co., Ltd.

NELSON, NICHOLAS and HAYES, J. JUEVAAL: "Trick Marionettes." Paul McPharlin, 155, Wimbleton Drive, Birmingham, Michigan, U.S.A.

JOSEPH, HELEN HAIMAN: " A Book of Marionettes." London: Allen & Unwin. Two editions.

CRAIG, E. GORDON: " Puppets and Poets." *The Chapbook, No.* 20. February, 1921. *See also Theatre Arts Monthly*, Special Marionette Number. July, 1928.

" Loutkar." The official organ of UNIMA, Prague. The series of illustrated booklets published by UNIMA on " The Most Important Marionette Theatres of the World ":

1. Prof. Anton Aicher. Salzburg.
2. Vittorio Podrecca. Rome.
3. Swiss Marionettes.
4. Czechoslovakia.
5. Richard Teschner. Vienna.
6. Roumanian Puppet Shows.

Foreign Marionettes, etc.

MARKS, HAYWARD J. W. and WHANSLAW, H. W. " Nigyo-shibai " (The Japanese Puppet Theatre). London: H. J. W. Marks, 65, Hosack Road, S.W. 17.

A description of the marionettes of Japan with one hand-tinted illustration and bibliography.

One of a series of handbooks dealing with Oriental and other Puppets.

BULLETT, G.: " Marionettes in Munich." *The Saturday Review.* December, 1929.

RACCA, CARLO: " Burratini e Marionette." G. B. Paravia & Co., Turin, Italy.

NOGUCHI, Y.: "The Japanese Puppet Theatre." *Arts and Decorations.* October, 1920.

GRÖBER, KARL: "Children's Toys of Bygone Days." London: B. T. Batsford.

VON TUSSENBROCK, OTTO: "De Togepaste Kunsten in Nederland." W. L. &. J. Brusse.

MIYAJIMA, T.: "Théâtre de Poupées." Kansai, 1926.
Histoire du Théâtre du Poupées.

MAGNIN, G.: "Histoire des Marionettes." 1852.
One of the finest histories of puppets in existence.

DE NEUVILLE, L.: "Histoire des Marionettes." 1892.

SEYFFERT, O. and TRIER, W.: "Spielzeug." Ernst Wasmuth, Berlin.

SCHINK, J. F.: "Marionetten Theatre." 1778.

MAHLMANN, S. A.: "Marionetten Theatre oder Sammlung." 1806.
These two old volumes of plays, etc., are in the British Museum Library.

JONES, H. FESTING: "Castellinaria" and "Diversions in Sicily" (Sicilian Marionettes). London: A. C. Fifield.

Der Puppenspieler. A German magazine, 1931-33. BOCHUM, SCHACHT.

Old Time Puppet Shows.

BOULTON, W. B.: "The Amusements of Old London." 1901.

CRAIG, E. GORDON: "History" of the Marionette Stage. "The Marionette" I. 1918 and following numbers.

PEIXOTTO, E. C.: "Marionettes and Puppet Shows Past and Present." Scribner's. 1903.

HONE, WILLIAM: "Ancient Mysteries Described." 1823.

" " "The Everyday Book."

STRUTT, JOSEPH: "The Sports and Pastimes of the People of England." 1838, etc.

JONSON, BEN: "Tale of a Tub" and "Bartholomew Fair."

Also in "Every Man out of His Humour" mention is made of Captain Pod, a famous puppet showman of his day.

DISRAELI, BENJAMIN: "Curiosities of Literature." Volume 3.

Punch and Judy

BARING, M.: "Punch and Judy." London: Mercury. July, 1922.

BOWIE, A. G.: "The Story of Punch and Judy." *The Theatre.* January, 1884.

BESSIER, F.: "Theàtre de Guignol."

WILKINSON, WALTER: "How to Make a Puppet Show." Dryad Handicrafts Leaflet No. 50. Leicester.

TOZER, H. V.: "The Puppet Theatre in Barcelona." "Puppetry." 1932.

MCPHARLIN, PAUL: "A Primer of Hand Puppets." Puppetry Handbook No. 4. Paul McPharlin, 155, Wimbleton Drive, Birmingham, Michigan, U.S.A.; Also "A Repertory of Marionette Plays," "Puppet Heads and their Making" and "Puppet Hands and their Making."

LAWRENCE, W. J.: "The Immortal Mr. Punch." *The Living Age*. January, 1921.

YIDDISH MARIONETTE THEATRE. *Theatre Arts Monthly*. June, 1926.

MARSARYK, L'INSTITUT: "Marionettes et Guignols in Tchécoslovaquie." Prague. 1930.

Scenic Art, etc.

FLETCHER, CAMPBELL: "Stage Craft." London: The C. W. Daniel Company.

DOLMAN, JOHN, JUNR.: "The Art of Play Production." London: Samuel French.

Rose, A.: "The Boy Showman and Entertainer." Samuel French.

Deals with marionettes, Punch and Judy, peep shows, etc.

Hartmann, Louis: "Theatre Lighting." Samuel French.

Rose, A.: "Stage Effects."

Brown, Van Dyke: "Secrets of Scene Painting and Stage Effects." London: George Routledge and Sons, Ltd.

Downs, Harold, edited by: "Theatre and Stage." London: Sir Isaac Pitman, Ltd.

This book contains a fine series of articles on stage effects by A. E. Peterson.

Costume

Stone, Melicent: "The Bankside Book of Costume." London: Wells Gardner, Darton and Co., Ltd.

Whanslaw, H. W.: "The Bankside Stage Book." London: Wells Gardner, Darton & Co., Ltd.

Fairholt: "Costume in England."

Calthrop, Dion Clayton: "English Costume." A. &. C. Black, Ltd.

Hottenroth, Fr.: "Le Costume." Paris: Armand Guérinet.
Over eleven hundred illustrations of costumes of all ages.

Ashdown, C. H.: "Arms and Armour." Edinburgh: T. C. & E. C. Jack.

SOCIETIES AND MARIONETTE FEDERATIONS

The British Puppet and Model Theatre Guild. *President:* Edward Gordon Craig, Esq. *Hon. Secretary:* Seymour Marks, 65, Hosack Road, London, S.W.17.

The Guild is registered as the British Federation of "Unima," the International Union of Marionettes, the aim of which is to unite makers, playwrights, performers, collectors and lovers of marionettes in all parts of the world. The Guild is therefore able to keep you informed of what is being done on the Continent and in America, as well as in this country.

The Marionette Theatre Guild. *Founder President:* J. T. Grein.

This society was formed in 1934 under the direction of Mr. J. T. Grein, the famous dramatic critic, Miss Margery Bryce, H. W. Whanslaw and W. S. Lanchester. The object is to produce from time to time first-class puppet productions by representative masters of all branches of the art.

10, Buckingham Street, Strand. London W.C.2.

UNIMA. Union Internationale des Marionettes. *President:* Dr. Jindřich Vesely, Prague, Czechoslovakia.

Holds a triennial conference and exhibition at which puppet workers from all over the world attend, and performances are given. UNIMA publishes the magazine of current and historical information, "Loutkar."

THE MARIONETTE FELLOWSHIP OF AMERICA. Affiliated with UNIMA. Founded 1930. *President:* Garret Becker. *General Secretary*: Max Shoher, 299, Broadway, New York City, U.S.A.

MATERIALS AND WHERE TO OBTAIN THEM

MARIONETTES AND PARTS—

The author will be pleased to give the names and addresses of first-class marionette and puppet makers to any who wish special figures constructed. All communications to H. W. Whanslaw, 7, Charlwood Terrace, Putney, S.W.15.

FIRE-PROOF WOOD (Beaver board, etc.)—

Any first-class wood-yard or builders' material suppliers.

CANVAS—

At a theatrical scene-cloth makers, Messrs. S. Witton & Co., 73, Oxford Street, Manchester.

ELECTRICAL FITTINGS—

The Strand Electric and Engineering Co., Ltd., 24, Floral Street, London, W.C.2.

Messrs. Thomas J. Digby, 12, Gerrard Street, London, W.1.

W. S. Lanchester, The Mews, Ravenscourt Gardens, W. 6.

GELATINES—

Messrs. Brodie & Middleton, Long Acre.

Strand Electric. See Electrical Fittings.

Messrs. Digby. " " "

CELASTOID—

The London Marionette Theatre, The Mews, Ravenscourt Gardens, Stamford Brook, W. 6.

BLUE PRINTS (to make seven inch, ten inch and eighteen inch marionettes)—

Professional "Travelling Fit-up."

CONTROLS, etc.—

The London Marionette Theatre.

RECORDS—

"Octacros," W. S. Lanchester.

"Permarec," Will Day, Musikon, Ltd., 19, Lisle Street, W.C. 2.

Other makers, H.M.V., Columbia, Regal, etc., from recognised dealers and music stores.

JAVANESE AND BURMESE PUPPETS—
Books, etc., dealing with Oriental marionettes. The Java Head Bookshop, Great Russell Street, W.C.2.

MARIONETTES IN LONDON MUSEUMS

VICTORIA AND ALBERT MUSEUM, South Kensington.
Antique Venetian Marionette Theatre, and case of additional marionettes.
Model Theatres in the collection of children's toys, and in the theatrical section.

INDIAN MUSEUM.
Javanese and Burmese marionettes of every description.

BRITISH MUSEUM, Great Russell Street, W.C.
Javanese marionettes.
Egyptian movable toys. Greek articulated dolls, etc.

GEFFRYE MUSEUM.
Marionettes, Javanese, etc.

Printed in the United Kingdom
by Lightning Source UK Ltd.
121570UK00001B/73/A

9 781406 799347